T0095330

# Developing Mental Toughness

*Teaching the Game of Life*

By

DR. TIMOTHY S. WAKEFIELD

www.developingmentaltoughness.com

authorHOUSE®

*AuthorHouse™*
*1663 Liberty Drive*
*Bloomington, IN 47403*
*www.authorhouse.com*
*Phone: 1-800-839-8640*

*© 2009 Dr. Timothy S. Wakefield. All Rights Reserved.*

*No part of this book may be reproduced, stored in a retrieval system, or transmitted by any means without the written permission of the author.*

*First published by AuthorHouse 4/27/2009*

*ISBN: 978-1-4389-7511-5 (sc)*

*Printed in the United States of America*
*Bloomington, Indiana*

*This book is printed on acid-free paper.*

Thank you to my loving wife, Dr. Lorelei N. Wakefield, for the guidance and assistance she provided in the development of this book. Thank you to my children for understanding the time commitment needed to accomplish this project and for (unknowingly) allowing me to use many of these techniques on them and watch their success. Thank you to my parents, Roger and Barbara Wakefield, for giving me the foundation to develop this project. Thank you to my friends and mentors who have assisted, encouraged, and coached me in this project.

# Contents

# *Purpose*

This book is about teaching life skills that many people assume will just be acquired. They will not be! In the employment arena, these skills have been called soft skills. The purpose of this program is to assist parents, grandparents, employers, coaches, teachers, and other instructors to help people deal with the successes and adversities that go with extending our self into employment, schools, extracurricular activities, and life. Many of the examples in this text are based on athletic events and then applied to life. The skills taught in this program can be applied to any venue we choose (in our home, at our job, in band, choir, athletic events, and in the classroom). This program is designed to develop life skills that people, both young and old, can use and apply for the rest of our lives. Mastering these skills will give you a huge advantage. If people are not taught these skills, either at home or in another setting, they will not be able to use them. Life skills are learned behaviors and must be taught in order to be used. Not learning, understanding, and applying these skills will limit success. Homes, camps, classrooms, extracurricular activities, and places of employment are opportune venues to teach and apply these life skills. People can then apply them to their everyday lives.

The more I'm involved with people of all ages, the less "competitive fire" I see in jobs, sports, extracurricular activities, and life. For people to be competitive, they must learn the skills to be competitive. To be successful in life, a person must learn how, when, where, and why to be competitive. Life is full of competition. Competition drives success and can be fun at the same time. Few people are taught how to compete in life with honor and dignity.

People of today appear to be much more intelligent than they were twenty or thirty years ago. As I was growing up, youths appeared much more physical. I have to believe that the pendulum swings both ways. We are raising our kids to be good kids. We want them to be polite and kind; we want them to achieve to their potential. Extracurricular activities and places of employment can be fantastic training grounds for the challenges that we may face in life. In an athletic competition for example, an athlete needs to think differently than a "good kid." Athletes need to learn it is okay and important to possess a competitive fire, intensity, and emotion to succeed in sports. These traits can then be carried into life. This behavior is learned and needs to be developed to succeed not only in sports, but in all areas of life.

Winning is the science of being totally prepared. We prepare our students with lessons in math, science, reading, and writing. We prepare athletes with skills training, weight training, agility, speed training, flexibility, offensive and defensive game plans. We teach our employees to do certain jobs and tasks. But overall, we do not do well at training them how to think, act, and behave to achieve success. Many of us do not do well training the soft skills of life. Many people feel these skills are just implied. It is something everyone should understand or it is just learned by watching others. We don't train them in the mental aspects of life success. Then we are frustrated with inappropriate behavior. We attempt to teach the mental and emotional components of school, employment, sports and life without organization. Many feel that these life skills are implied, meaning that they should just know it, "It is common sense". To many, it is not common sense. Quite frankly, many do not understand that they need to act a certain way to get a certain result. This program is designed to train the mental and emotional aspects of life in a systematic and organized manner.

It is my hope that implementing *Developing Mental Toughness: Teaching the Game of Life* will provide parents, teachers, coaches, employers, and all other instructors with an organized, systematic approach for teaching the mental and emotional components of life. Teaching this program can give you, your children, students, players, and employees the mental and emotional tools for success in life. Mental toughness is the missing link to true success in schools, athletics, employment, and life.

This program is designed to assist in teaching people how to deal with the different emotions and situations necessary to experience optimum success in life. How can we accomplish such a feat? It is my hope that the lessons set forth in *Developing Mental Toughness: Teaching the Game of Life* will give guidance and structure in training people to have successful, happy, and fulfilling lives. They can then pass this down to their children and grandchildren. It is my hope that this book will assist people in developing the competitive fire needed to succeed in life and assist them in handling all the challenges and opportunities life has to offer.

Training in the physical, mental, and emotional aspects of success will give all a greater chance of succeeding in life.

Good luck!

# Getting the Most Out of This Book

A Special Note to Parents, Teachers, Coaches, Employers and other Instructors

My experience teaches me there are two critical criteria that make this program successful. First, there must be a consistent format from which to teach these concepts. By following the format in this book, the lessons are teachable and learnable. Second is repetition. These traits must be taught over and over again. A good format to use is *Teach them, teach them what you taught them, and then teach them again.*

## How to Use This Program

I recommend that each person have and use one of these manuals. Write in this book. Mark it up, and use it for years to come. The instructor may start at the beginning and teach each lesson in order, or he or she may teach each lesson in a manner determined by the specific needs.

I recommend that this program be taught consistently and that both the instructors and the students write in these manuals. I am often asked when to implement the program. There are many options: the first five minutes of each class, practice, or job, on Mondays, during staff or employment meetings and so on. Any time is good; just try to be consistent and teach it over and over again. The student should answer all questions in the format that is outlined. The information is then handed in to the instructor for review. There is no right answer; this is used strictly as a training device. It is beneficial for the instructor to enforce the information discussed in terms of the answers given by specific students. For example: "When we spoke about desire just two weeks ago, one of you wrote in your outline that desire is giving 100 percent. Do you feel you are giving 100 percent now? Do you feel others around you are giving 100 percent? Let's do this with the desire to do your best."

*Developing mental toughness* will provide parents, coaches, teachers, employers and other instructors with a framework for teaching the mental aspects of *life.*

# Life Lessons

*If we don't risk anything, we risk it all.*

It is important to understand that not all life lessons are pleasant. Lessons learned have the ability to catapult people ahead in life. The more life experiences we have when we are young, the more we are able to deal with the adversities and opportunities that life may send us. The more we are allowed to fight our own battles, the stronger we will become for the life battles ahead, especially when no one is there to fight the battles for us. This is the beauty of participating in extracurricular activities when we are young. It assists us in learning about dealing with ourselves and others. These activities can expose us to difficult times, disappointment, hard work, and happiness—some of the key ingredients in learning to appreciate life.

# <u>Life</u>

*No one can do it for us.*
*We have no one to blame but ourselves.*
*The answers are buried somewhere deep inside our soul.*

*We did not ask to be here but we are.*
*We have one chance to be the best we can be.*

*Are you prepared?*
*Have you trained both mind and body?*

*This is no walk in the park.*
*This is our life.*
*The most intense sport on earth.*

# Lesson One: The Mental Law of Success

*Ideas we can think of, believe in, and confidently
expect of ourselves must become our experience.*

Explanation:

1. The *inside* of our head determines the *outside* of our life. Our thoughts and feelings attract our life to us. The way we look at the world is the way the people of the world will look back at us.

2. We are how we think.
    a. If we think positive thoughts, we will have a positive life.
    b. If we think negative thoughts, we will have a negative life.
    c. If we are critical of ourselves and other people, we will attract more of what we are critical about.
    d. If we say something negative about someone else, it will come back to haunt us.
    e. Garbage in, garbage out!
    f. Greatness in, greatness out!

3. We are, right now, where our minds have been in the past.

4. By changing our minds, we can change their effects.
    a. If we think something won't work, it won't.
    b. We can't do something if we think we can't.

5. Our thoughts and beliefs control our lives.
    a. What we think and believe is what we will get out of life.
    b. Whether we think we can or think we can't—we are right.

6. Our thoughts must be backed up by physical action in order to succeed.
   a. Control your mind, and add physical action to control your success.

This is commonly called mental toughness. Mental toughness allows us to keep focused and not be distracted by outside influences that may take us off course. This includes family, friends, teachers, employers, fellow employees, teammates, referees or officials, fans, and coaches. We have control over the way we think, and the way that we think *will* control our destiny. If you allow stinking thinking, you will be stinking. If you choose to think like a champion, you will become a champion. It is truly up to us. Our thoughts control our destiny, and we control our thoughts. Positive thinking is the hope that we can move mountains. Positive believing is the same hope, but with a reason for believing we can do it.

Examples of real-life applications:

Instructor: Give an example of how this lesson could apply to your life, family, or job. If you feel yourself thinking destructive thoughts, how do you change it?

How does the Mental Law of Success apply to you?

If you have stinking thinking, what do you have to do to change it?

How could the Mental Law of Success apply to a team or group?

How could you apply the Mental Law of Success in school or on the job?

How could you apply the Mental Law of Success at your home?

How could you apply the Mental Law of Success to your life in the future?

*We are today where our minds have been in the past. We can change what we are, who we are, and where we are by changing what goes on between our ears. Changing what we think and how we think can change our world!*

# Lesson Two: *The Physical Law of Success*

*We must think it, see it, hear it, touch it, and do it to achieve it.*

Explanation:

1. We are as good right now as we've *really* wanted to be in the past.

2. The more physical energy we put into something, the more we will get out of it.

3. Nothing can prevent us from having what we sincerely desire, as long as we are willing to put out the physical effort to attain it.

   a. If you want to be stronger, work on your strength.
   b. If you want to be faster, work on your speed.
   c. If you want to be better at a skill, work on that skill.
   d. If you want to be smarter, study more.
   e. If you want others to respect you, respect others.
   f. If you want others to be polite to you, be polite to others.
   g. If you want to have a friend, be a friend.

4. No good effort is ever wasted.

5. The harder you work, the harder it becomes for others to defeat you.

6. The harder you work, the harder it is for you to surrender.

7. The harder you work, the luckier you get!

Luck is when preparation meets opportunity.

The best compliment you can receive is if people call you lucky. Work hard, and people may call you lucky. Where were these people when you were preparing for the opportunities of the future? Where they watching TV, playing video games and sleeping in when you were waking up early, going to the weight room, and working on your skills? Luck is when preparation meets opportunity. This applies to all areas of life.

How do you create your luck?

In school this means to:

- Show up to class on time
- Be teachable
- Listen
- Ask appropriate questions
- Take notes
- Do your home work and hand it in on time
- Study
- Get help when needed
- Be respectful, honest, and hard working
- Help others if they ask

In employment this means to:

- Show up on time for work
- Be willing to listen and take instruction
- Ask questions if you do not understand
- Be respectful, honest and hard working
- Do the best you can  (Your work is a reflection of you)
- Ask for help if needed
- Hustle while you work
- After you get your job done, help others

In athletics, this means to:

- Weight train
- Develop foot speed
- Work on agility
- Work on flexibility and endurance
- Watch film
- Be coach-able
- Work on the fundamentals of the sport
- Eat well
- Be honest
- Have high integrity

- Be respectful
- Help others succeed

We must prepare for our opportunities, and then take advantage of them.

Examples of real-life applications:

Instructor: Give an example of how this lesson could apply to your life, family, or job.

How does the Physical Law of Success apply to you?

How could the Physical Law of Success apply to a team or group?

How could you apply the Physical Law of Success in school or on the job?

How could you apply the Physical Law of Success at your home?

How could you apply the Physical Law of Success to your life in the future?

*Hustling while we wait will create great opportunity!*

# Lesson Three: The Law of Human Behavior

*If we give our very best effort, we will never regret the outcome.*
*Every job we perform is a portrait of our life.*
*What portrait are you painting?*

<u>Explanation:</u>

Behavior is our conduct or actions. Our behavior is how we act under certain circumstances. Human behavior can be an interesting topic. The way we behave demonstrates what we truly want, not what we say we want, out of life.

There are four primary components to human behavior. All four affect each other and influence your behavior.

1. *Thoughts*: Our thoughts develop our actions and feelings, and they influence our body function (our physiology). Positive thoughts develop different actions, feelings, and physiology than negative thoughts. Positive thoughts create good feelings about ourselves and others. Positive thoughts create positive actions and the physiology to build a strong, healthy body. Negative thoughts do the opposite.

2. *Physical Actions*: Our actions reinforce our thoughts, validate our feelings, and stimulate additional physiology reinforcing that thought.

3. *Feelings and emotions*: Our feelings and emotions are controlled by our reaction to our surroundings. Our feelings influence our actions, our thoughts, and our physiology.

4. *Physiology*: Our body releases different chemicals, such as hormones, in response to our thoughts, actions, and feelings. These influence our physiology and can influence our health. Positive experiences create health, and negative experiences inhibit health (create disease). Research has shown that prolonged negative thoughts develop poor physiological effects such as anxiety, depression, and cancer. With positive thoughts, we can help to eliminate these types of diseases.

The Law of Human Behavior: Sooner or later, we get exactly what we expect. Some people view this statement as positive; others view it as negative. The people who see this as an optimistic or positive statement generally see the world more positively. Those who see this as a pessimistic or negative statement generally see the negatives of the world. Our thoughts are our choices. When looking at our future, we must ask ourselves, "What do I want, and what do I expect of myself to accomplish it?" What are we going to do, and how do we expect to behave to meet our expectations? We must have expectations of ourselves to achieve in any area of our life. Our expectations of ourselves will mold our lives. Some people's behaviors destroy their own dreams. Some people's behaviors support and assist in developing their dreams.

Example: Two people may have the dream of playing college baseball.

Person one awakes four days per week at 5:20 a.m. and goes to the weight room at 6:00 a.m. There he works on his strength, flexibility, endurance, coordination, agility, hitting, and fielding until 7:30 a.m. He also goes to baseball camps, stays after practice to work on individual skills, watches film of himself and others, and meets with the coach to help him find colleges.

Person two awakes just in time to get to school, shows up to practice, and does not weight train or do any additional training besides what is required by the coach.

Which person is behaving like he wants to play college baseball? Which person will probably have a better chance of playing college baseball?

Person one is dedicated. He is making the sacrifices needed to play college baseball. He is behaving like a college baseball player.

Person two is just giving lip service to playing college baseball. This person may have the talent, but not the dedication. He is not behaving like a college baseball player.

Every job that we perform is a portrait of us. If we give our best effort, we will never regret the outcome. Without 100 percent commitment to doing what we want, there is no commitment at all.

If you like where you are and what you are doing in life, then continue to do that and grow. If we want to change our life and our destiny, we must change our thoughts, actions, feelings, and physiology. If we do this, it will change our behavior. This will change our destiny and our life.

We must think we can (the Mental Law of Success), add physical action (the Physical Law of Success), and then behave like we can (the Law of Human Behavior) to achieve. This can be applied to every situation in our lives.

Examples of real-life applications:

Instructor: Give an example of how this lesson could apply to your life, family, or job. What do you expect of yourself?

How does the Law of Human Behavior apply to you?

How could the Law of Human Behavior apply to a team or group?

How could you apply the Law of Human Behavior in school or on the job?

How could you apply the Law of Human Behavior at your home?

How could you apply the Law of Human Behavior to your life in the future?

*Success is achieved by following through with a consistent series of small, positive, thoughts, actions, and behaviors.*

# Lesson Four: The Spiritual Law of Success

*One way or another we get paid back for everything we do.*

Explanation:

1. Everything we do comes back to us.
   a. If we give good, we will receive good.
   b. If we give bad, we will receive bad.

2. We will always get paid back for what we do, one way or another (some claim we are repaid tenfold).

3. Do not do what you would undo if caught. Our consequence is the "playback" of the small voice within us that warned us not to do it in the first place.

4. What can we do to help others and ourselves?

Examples of real-life applications:

Instructor: Give an example of how this lesson could apply to your life, family, or job.

How does the Spiritual Law of Success apply to you?

How could the Spiritual Law of Success apply to a team or group?

How could you apply the Spiritual Law of Success in school or on the job?

How could you apply the Spiritual Law of Success at your home?

How could you apply the Spiritual Law of Success to your life in the future?

*Our thoughts and actions develop our lives.*

# Life Is a Game
# And
# You Make the Rules

*Life is a game and you make the rules.*
*There are no winners. There are no losers.*
*At times you will win; at times you will lose.*
*Winning and losing are normal in life and teach us lessons.*
*Learn from those lessons.*

*Grab on to the wins.*
*Let go of your losses.*
*Move onto the next game.*

*There will be peaks and valleys in life.*
*Hang on to the peaks as long as you can.*
*Crawl out of the valleys as fast as you can.*
*Do not let the valleys of life crush your spirit.*
*Move through the valleys of life anticipating the next great thing that will*
*happen to you.*
*It will.*

*Life is a game and you make the rules.*
*You are your own Santa Claus.*
*You are your own Wizard.*

*Life is a game and you make the rules.*
*Are you winning your game of life?*

# Lesson Five: The Law of Self-Talk

*Are you your own worst enemy or biggest fan?*

Explanation:

Self-talk is the daily mental conversation we have with ourselves. What do you think about you?

How we talk to ourselves influences how we will think, act, and behave. Our self-talk can single-handedly shape our destiny.

If I talked to you the way many of you talk to yourselves—you would hate me.

Self-talk changes thoughts and thoughts change lives.

Think "why not" instead of "can't."

Think "abundance" instead of "lack."

What are you going to be? Are you going to be an average person? An average person is the best of the worst and the worst of the best. Average is not like you. Be the best you can be.

One thought can change a life. One positive thought thrown away or forgotten could be the thought that changes our lives. A short pencil is better than a long memory. Write down your great thoughts and keep them for the future.

Self-talk will build or destroy our self-esteem. *Positive* self-talk will build our self-esteem. Until we have great self-esteem, we cannot truly love another person.

How do we build positive self-talk? By controlling how we talk to ourselves.

How do we control how we talk to ourselves?

- Figure out solutions; do not dwell on problems.
- Recognize the good in the world, not the bad.
- Think of opportunities, not tragedies.

Talk in a positive way to yourself.
- I am good.
- Good things happens to me.
- I deserve good things.
- I create good for myself and others.

Our thoughts are our habits. Develop the habit of positive self-talk.

Get excited about yourself and your life! You've got great opportunities ahead of you! You are a great person! People like you!

Our future starts with how we think of ourselves. How we think is a choice. Negative thoughts hold us back. Positive thoughts propel us into the future. Get excited about you! You are awesome, you are smart, and you are happy. People like you and want to be around you; young people want to be like you! If we believe in ourselves, have a dream, use positive self-talk, add physical action and behave like it is going to happen — we will achieve. With positive self-talk we can bring out the best in the world!

Examples of real-life applications:

Instructor: Give an example of how this lesson could apply to your life, family, or job.

How does self-talk apply to you?

How could self-talk apply to a team or group?

How could you apply self-talk in the school or on the job?

How could you apply self-talk at your home?

How could you apply self-talk to your life in the future?

*A person will achieve to the level they believe.*
*How we talk to ourselves can control our destinies.*

# The Sand in the Glass

*Each day we have an opportunity to get closer to our goals. Everything we do either gets us closer to, or further from, our goals and dreams. The law of momentum says there is only a split second when we are stopped. We are either moving forward or backward. It is up to us.*

*I like to explain this to athletes like this: In high school, our athletic potential is like a glass. Just as everyone's athletic potential is different, so is the size of our glass. Everything we do to get better is like adding a grain of sand to our glass. We hope that when we are a high school senior our glass is overflowing with sand. Then we have reached our high school athletic potential. If we are fortunate enough to be asked to play college athletics, we take our glass, empty it into an ice cream pail, and start filling it up again—one grain of sand at a time. We hope to have that ice cream pail filled and overflowing by the time we are a college senior. If we are fortunate enough to be asked to be a professional athlete, we take that ice cream pail, dump it into a five-gallon bucket, and again start the process of adding grains of sand to that bucket. We hope to be able to fill it.*

*What we do on a daily basis determines if we are adding to our sand container. In athletics, these things consist of weight training, agility training, strength and speed training, watching film, coordination, balance training, and training in mental toughness. Also included is communication, leadership, academics, goal setting, team building, and nutritional and sleep habits. Work ethic, honesty, integrity, respect, and being coach-able are also important.*

*Some people are self-destroyers. After all their hard word of putting sand in their container, they consciously or unconsciously reach in and remove sand. Some knock over their own containers, destroying the opportunities they have created for themselves. They do this with the life choices they make. They may smoke, drink, or take illegal drugs. They may fail a class, get into a fight, break the law, abuse another person, or talk back to a coach, parent, or teacher. They may choose to be cruel, disrespectful, or dishonest. They may point out the weaknesses in others, have poor integrity, or boast about their accomplishments. These are just a few things that can negatively affect our lives and abilities.*

*Many of these positive and negative traits will determine the level of success or failure we achieve in our future career and relationships and as a person in general. These are the life choices we make. This is another reason why I love extra-curricular activities; they can train us for life!*

# *Lesson Six: Goal Setting and Planning*

*Goal setting and planning are vital to appreciating life's successes.*

Explanation:

People who teach the principles of success understand that goal setting and planning are vital components to achieving one's dreams. It is estimated that less than 5 percent of people set clear, concise, written goals. That means that 95 percent of people are either too lazy, too busy, or don't care enough to develop their futures.

I ask you this: What goals would you set, if you *knew* you could not fail? What type of life would you build? Fear is one thing that can hold us all back. There is nothing to fear but fear itself. Would it be better to fail to achieve an outlandish goal that could positively change the people of the world, or to have no goal at all?

*Have goals, will travel!* If we fail to plan, it is a plan to fail. What goals would you set, if you knew you could not fail? These are the goals you need to set! Goals will remove self-imposed limitations from our life. A person may not always make his or her goals, but the goals will always make the person. If we aim at nothing, we will always succeed. If we never risk anything, we risk everything.

After a few losses, we are sometimes afraid to try. What are the two most difficult parts of anything? Getting it started and keeping it going. Keep this in mind: a thousand-mile journey starts with the first step and we get closer with each step we take.

Remember:

- Things must change.
- Enjoy change.
- Change is fun.

- Goal setting and planning create change.
- Change makes us happy.

 Goal setting and planning is the process of achieving and appreciating our life. Goal setting and planning can be very complicated, or it can be easy. It generally depends on the goal being set. There are some fundamental steps with setting a goal. We must figure out something we want to accomplish, set goals, and make a plan to succeed. When setting goals, remember:

1.  Goals must be realistic, but only to you. Do not let others' limitations destroy your goal.

2.  Goals must be attainable, but only to you. Do not allow others to put obstacles in your way.

3.  Goals must be measurable. We must know when we have reached our goal.

After we have figured out the steps we must take to reach our goal, then make the plan:

1.  Write your goals on a piece of paper.

2.  Write a date after each goal, so you know when you are to achieve that goal.

3.  Under the goal, right down what you have to do to achieve that goal.

4.  Read this out loud three to five times a day.

5.  Take action to fulfill your goals and dreams.

6.  Never give up.

Example:

Dream: I want to be a Certified Public Accountant (CPA) by_____(date).

Goal one: I want to get a 3.5 grade point average (GPA) by_____ (date). Write it on an index card you will carry with you all the time, along with your outlined plan:

1.  I will learn good study habits by_____(date)
2.  I will partner with teacher X to assist me in putting together a program to help me reach my goal of a 3.5 GPA by_____(date).
3.  I will have a 3.5 GPA on or before _____(date).
4.  I will read this out loud three to five times per day.
5.  I will not give up.

Goal two: I will choose the college I will attend by_____ (date).

1.  I will meet with my school counselor by_____ (date).
2.  I will start college visits by_____ (date).
3.  I will visit three colleges by_____(date).
4.  I will review financial aid options by_____(date).

In order to attain our goals, we must think of it, physically do something about it, believe it can happen, behave like it is happening, positively talk to ourselves about it, and confidently expect it of ourselves. Remember, if the going gets easier, we are not climbing. If we are not climbing, we are probably falling. Just like a ball that is thrown directly above you stops for a very short period of time before falling, we only stop for a short period of time before falling. Keep our momentum going forward and continue to strive for excellence in all that you do.

Many training programs about goal setting are available. To achieve a goal, write it, read it, hear it, feel it with emotion, and act on it. This will give us the motivation and the passion to reach our goal. Once we set a goal, accomplish it—even if obstacles get in the way.

>   *Expect the best, prepare for the worst, and take advantage of what develops.*
>   *Establishing a goal and being committed to it will positively change our lives.*

Examples of real-life applications:

Instructor: Give an example of how this lesson could apply to your life, family, or job.

How does goal setting and planning apply to you?

How could goal setting and planning apply to a team or group?

How could you apply goal setting and planning in school or on the job?

How could you apply goal setting and planning at your home?

How could you apply goal setting and planning to your life in the future?

*Having a goal is the most important step towards success.*

*If we take a train off its tracks, it is free, but it cannot go anywhere. Goals are the tracks that lead us to our destination.*

# Who are your partners?

*We live in northern Wisconsin, 100 (or more) miles from any major city. My wife and I are both doctors of chiropractic. On July 26, 2008 I received a call that every parent fears. It was a Saturday just before noon. I came into the clinic that morning to treat a few patients. I called home to see if anyone needed anything before I came home for the weekend. I was told by a friend that my 12 year-old son had an ATV accident in the woods. They were just leaving to check on him. I felt like someone kicked me in the stomach. I dropped everything and rushed home.*

*When I got to the scene he was lying on the seat of his ATV on his back with his hands on his forehead and his feet on the gas tank. His lower back was sore but he was able to walk and appeared to have normal strength in his legs. We got him off the ATV, he walked to my truck and we took him to our clinic for x-rays. The x-rays were taken, and our hearts sank. We called the ER, and the MD said to get him there as soon as possible. It appeared our son had fractured his low back. He was transferred by helicopter to one hospital. They took an MRI and decided they were not equipped to handle such a severe injury and they would have to transfer him by helicopter to the UW Children's Hospital in Madison, Wisconsin.*

*By the time we all arrived in Madison it was approximately 1:00 a.m. During this time he did not have a lot of pain. He had sensation and could move his legs, but his legs would ache. I was very concerned that the fracture site or swelling would choke off his spinal cord, and he would end up with permanent damage. At approximately 1:00 p.m. he had surgery reducing the dislocation and fusing the fracture site with two metal plates and four screws. According to the surgeon, this could have taken up to four hours. After two hours the doctor contacted us explaining the surgery went better than expected, and they would be returning him back to his room. He was to remain on his back until he was fit for his body cast that they call a turtle shell. He was fitted for the turtle shell a few hours later, and the turtle shell was made and delivered the following day. The turtle shell was placed on him, and he was able to take his first few steps. I cried when I could see my son walk and use all his bodily functions.*

*He was in his turtle shell for ten weeks. During this time we assisted his healing with chiropractic treatment, proper nutrition, low-level laser therapy, and exercise to maintain strength, flexibility, coordination and balance. Ten weeks later he saw the surgeon. The surgeon felt he was healing well, and when we determined that he had strengthened his core body muscles (stomach and back muscles), he could return to non-contact sporting events such as basketball. He played his first basketball game on October 27, 2008.*

*In this time of major catastrophe, who did we partner with? We partnered with many. We partnered with the hospitals, the EMT's, the helicopter pilots, the doctors, the nurses, the medical assistants, the turtle shell makers, the physical therapists, the janitors, the cafeteria personnel, the people who built my car, the gas stations, the people who took over our chiropractic clinic while we were gone, our staff, our instructors that trained us in chiropractic and rehabilitation, our friends and family, etc. We partnered with many people during this catastrophic event. We partner with many people every day. Partnering is a necessary part of life.*

# Lesson Seven: Partnering

*Once we think we know it all—we don't.*
*Smart people learn by their experience.*
*Wise people learn by the experience of others.*

Explanation:

In order to reach our goals, we may need the help of other people. This is called "partnering." A component of partnering is recruiting the help of other people to assist us in achieving our goals and dreams. Life involves a lot of partnering. We may partner with a teacher to maintain our grades. We may partner with a seminar to develop knowledge about our job. We may partner with a CPA to help us with our taxes. We may partner with the strength and conditioning coach to increase our strength or speed. There are many areas in life where we consciously or unconsciously partner with others to assist us in achievement.

If we find an area of weakness or establish a goal that we need help to achieve, it is important to ask for the assistance of others. Many times, people will freely and graciously help us to achieve our goals. None of us have all the answers. It is important to partner with the people who may have those answers. Use the knowledge of others to help you to achieve your goals.

We partner with others in many areas of our lives, from going to the grocery store for weekly shopping to hiring accountants and attorneys to put together complicated business deals. Many people are hesitant to ask others for help, but in reality, we are all dependent on others to achieve our goals. Most people are willing to help—just ask.

*If we are willing to help others get what they want, we can have everything that we want. Get partners and become a partner.*

Partnering Project

Name five people whom you need to help you do what *you* want to do. Write down what they do for you. Lastly, thank them, either verbally or with a quick note or card. This is appreciation. For example:

| Name | What They Do for You | Appreciation |
|---|---|---|
| 1. Mrs. Smith | Teaches me math | Sent thank-you card |
| 2. Mr. Johnson | Is a janitor at my work | Gave a special thank-you |
| 3. Mrs. Peterson | Washes our team uniforms | Told her I appreciated her |

1.

2.

3.

4.

5.

Examples of real-life applications:

Instructor: Give an example of how this lesson could apply to your life, family, or job.

How does partnering apply to you?

How could partnering apply to a team or group?

How could you apply partnering in school or on the job?

How could you apply partnering at your home?

How could you apply partnering to your life in the future?

*We partner with many; it is important to appreciate them.*

# Lesson Eight: Dreaming Big Dreams

*Before we can get what we want out of life, we have to decide
what we want out of life.*

Explanation:

A dream (in this context) is a thought that others may see as unrealistic, but is one that you are driven to accomplish.

Many people do not realize that before we can accomplish anything, we have to dream about it. We have to be able to think that we can do something before we can do it. If we are going to dream, why not dream big? If we dream small and only accomplish small things, then we are limiting our ability to grow. Dreams are free. Dream big dreams; set our goals high, and start a plan to accomplish them. Be disciplined in accomplishing your plan in order for your dreams to come true. Shooting high and missing your mark is better than shooting low and hitting our mark. When we hit a low mark, it means we could have done more.

That which we can dream of, believe in, and confidently expect of ourselves must become our experience. If we don't have a dream, how are we going to have a dream come true?

Be satisfied with your accomplishments and dream big dreams. If we are satisfied with yesterday's accomplishments, we have done nothing yet today.

Would you rather shoot for the stars and land on the moon, or shoot for the moon and land on the barn? We all have greatness within us. We all have great dreams within us. We will all get kicked when going after our dreams—that is normal. Would you rather attempt something great and fail, or do nothing and succeed? Dreams can change the world. *Your* dream can change the world. The hardest step in accomplishing anything is the first step. The first step is to have a dream. If you are going to have a dream, why not have a big dream?

*Dreamers are happy people.*
*Dreamers can see the future.*
*Dreamers are fun to be around.*
*Dreams can change the world.*

Examples of real-life applications:

Instructor: Give an example of how this lesson could apply to your life, family, or job.

How does dreaming big dreams apply to you?

How could dreaming big dreams apply to a team or group?

How could you apply dreaming big dreams in school or on the job?

How could you apply dreaming big dreams at your home?

How could you apply dreaming big dreams to your life in the future?

*Do not let others' reality destroy your dream. Let your dream destroy their reality.*

# ACCOMPLISHING YOUR DREAMS

*Simple Thoughts to Consider When Striving for Your Dreams:*

*1. You may have many dreams you want to accomplish.
What is one of your dreams?*

*2. How must you think to accomplish your dream?
(Mental Law of Success)*

*3. What must you expect of yourself to accomplish your dream?
(Law of Human Behavior)*

*4. What must you physically do to accomplish your dream?
(Physical Law of Success)*

*5. What good must you create to accomplish your dream?
(Spiritual Law of Success)*

*6. What goals must you attain to accomplish your dream? Identify a plan to
accomplish the goals.
(goal setting and planning)*

*7. Whom must you partner with to achieve your dream?
(partnering)*

*8. How must you talk to yourself to accomplish your dream?
(Law of Self-Talk)*

Name:_____        Date:_____

## Dream Accomplishment Worksheet

*Success is not afraid of sacrifice.*
*If we can dream it and confidently expect it of ourselves, we can make it come true.*

My dream is to: _____

I will accomplish my dream on or before: _____ (date)

A *wish* is a thought or concept that we would like to have happen, but we are not willing to do what it takes to make it happen. We may want a wish for a while, but then we easily let it go.

A *dream* is a burning desire so deep inside our soul that we are willing to sacrifice and do whatever it takes to accomplish it. There will be obstacles when accomplishing any dream. When an obstacle is in our way, we have four options: go over it, go around it, go under it, or blow it up. There are many ways to accomplish our dream. It is important to write down our dream and the steps we need to take to achieve our dream. It is important to review our steps often. This will keep us on track to accomplish our dream. Many people spend more time putting a grocery list together than they do planning their own lives. Some people plan a trip by making lists of things to bring, planning where they will stay, planning events or entertainment, and reading a map on how to get there. But they forget to plan the most important thing they will ever have—*their lives*.

This Dream Accomplishment Worksheet will use the following fundamentals to assist you in planning and accomplishing your dream:

1. The Mental Law of Success
2. Goal setting and planning
3. The Physical Law of Success
4. Partnering
5. The Spiritual Law of Success
6. The Law of Human Behavior
7. The Law of Self-Talk

1. The Mental Law of Success

The inside of your head determines the outside of your life. Your thoughts and feelings attract your life to you. The way you look at the world is the way the people of the world look back at you. Your thoughts and beliefs control your life. You have control over the way you think. The way you think will control your destiny. If you choose to think like a champion, even when it is difficult to think like a champion, you will become a champion. Your thoughts control your destiny, and you control your thoughts.

List five ways you must think in order to accomplish your goal:

    1. I must think I can _____

    2. I must be confident I can _____

    3. I must work through obstacles when trying to _____

    4. I must think I can partner with _____

    5. _____

## 2. Goal setting and planning

*If we fail to plan, it is a plan to fail.*

You may have to accomplish many goals to achieve your dream. Goals will change and become clearer as you get closer to accomplishing your dream. List five goals you must accomplish to achieve your dream. In the future, list more goals as they become clearer.

Goal                                                                     Date

    1. _____

    2. _____

    3. _____

    4. _____

    5. _____

## 3. The Physical Law of Success

Your thoughts must be backed up by physical action in order to succeed. First, control your mind. Then add physical action to control your success. Establish your plan by identifying what you need to do and how you are going to do it.

Apply the Physical Law of Success to accomplishing your dream.

    1. List your five goals on the corresponding goal lines below.

    2. List *what* you must physically do to accomplish this goal. If there is not enough room, use another sheet of paper.

    3. List *how* you are going to physically accomplish this.

Example:

Goal: I will have a 3.5 grade point average (GPA) by _____ (date).

What: I will meet with my teachers to figure out what I can do to increase my GPA.

How: I will study daily, get all my homework done and do all extra credit.

1. Goal: _____
   What: _____
   How: _____

2. Goal: _____
   What: _____
   How: _____

3. Goal:
   What: _____
   How: _____

4. Goal: _____
   What: _____
   How: _____

5. Goal: _____
   What: _____
   How: _____

4. Partnering

Partnering is identifying the people you may need to assist you in accomplishing your goals and dreams.

List three people or things you must partner with to accomplish your goals and dreams. List the "who or what" you will partner with and what they could help you with. List the purpose of you partnering with that person or entity, and list three questions you would want to ask that person or entity.

Example:

Goal: I will have a 3.5 GPA by _____.

Who/what: Teachers

I will partner with: _____.

Purpose: To improve my GPA to a 3.5 or better.

Three questions:

   What are some things I can do to increase my grades?
   Is there any extra credit I can do?
   If I have questions about my schoolwork, what are the best ways to get them answered?

Goal 1:_____
Who/what I will partner with: _____
Purpose: _____
Three questions:
   1._____
   2._____
   3._____

Goal 2:_____
Who/what I will partner with:_____
Purpose:_____
Three questions:
   1._____
   2._____
   3._____

Goal 3:_____
Who/what I will partner with:_____
Purpose:_____
Three questions:
   1._____
   2._____
   3._____

Goal 4:_____
Who/what I will partner with:_____
Purpose:_____
Three questions:
   1._____
   2._____
   3._____

Goal 5:_____

Who/what I will partner with:_____

Purpose:_____

Three questions:

        1._____

        2._____

        3._____

5. The Spiritual Law of Success

Everything you do comes back to you. If you put out good, you will receive good. One way or another, you are always repaid for what you do.

Using the Spiritual Law of Success, list five things you can do to help others. This will attract benefits to you as you work on your dream.

Example:

Dream: I will become a doctor of chiropractic.

        1. I will read and learn about chiropractic.

        2. I will see the good in other people and make a point of telling them.

        3. I will volunteer in a chiropractic office to learn how to communicate with patients.

        4. I will volunteer at the Special Olympics to learn how to interact with people with special needs.

        5. I will ask my teachers for extra credit in the areas of human biology and communication.

My Dream:_____

List five good things that you can do to help you achieve your dream (Spiritual Law of Success):

    1._____

_____

    2._____

_____

    3._____

_____

    4._____

_____

    5._____

_____

## 6. The Law of Human Behavior

Sooner or later, you get exactly what you expect. What do you expect of yourself as far as accomplishing your dreams? Your goals are the steps you take to accomplish your dreams. How do you expect yourself to meet your goals and accomplish your dreams? What are your expectations for *yourself*?

List five things you expect of yourself to help accomplish your goals:

1. I expect myself to become _____

2. I expect myself to partner with _____

3. I expect myself to physically _____

4. I expect myself to behave like _____

5. I expect myself to _____

## 7. The Law of Self-Talk

The way we talk to ourselves is the way we will think and behave. Our self-talk can single-handedly shape our destinies. Be your own biggest fan! Self-talk truly changes lives. How must you talk to yourself to accomplish your dream?

1. _____

2. _____

3. _____

4. _____

5. _____

6. _____

*Our destiny is determined by choice, not chance.*

# Dream Accomplishment Map

*Action will eliminate fear, so step into action now.*

*Be careful—if we accept anything besides the very best, we will very likely get it.*

Dream: _____

The Mental Law of Success
I must think I can: _____
_____

Goal setting and planning
List the goal, the date by which it will be accomplished, what you will do, how you will do it, and who/what you will partner with.

I will achieve these five goals in order to accomplish my dream.

1. Goal: _____ by ____/____/_____
To accomplish this, I will: _____
_____

How I will do this: _____
_____

I will partner with: _____
For the purpose of: _____
I will ask these three questions:

1._____
_____

2. _____
_____

3._____
_____

2. Goal: _____ by ___/___/___
To accomplish this, I will: _____
_____

How I will do this: _____
_____

I will partner with: _____
For the purpose of: _____
I will ask these three questions:

1._____
_____

2. _____
_____

3._____
_____

3. Goal: _____ by ___/___/___
To accomplish this, I will: _____
_____

How I will do this: _____
_____

I will partner with: _____
For the purpose of: _____
I will ask these three questions:

1._____
_____

2. _____
_____

3._____
_____

4. Goal: _____ by ____/____/_____

To accomplish this, I will: _____

_____

How I will do this: _____

_____

I will partner with: _____

For the purpose of: _____

I will ask these three questions:

1._____

_____

2._____

_____

3._____

_____

5. Goal: _____ by ____/____/_____

To accomplish this, I will: _____

_____

How I will do this: _____

_____

I will partner with: _____

For the purpose of: _____

I will ask these three questions:

1._____

_____

2._____

_____

3._____

_____

The Spiritual Law of Success

I will do the following good deeds to assist me in accomplishing my goal:

1. _____
2. _____
3. _____
4. _____
5. _____

The Law of Human Behavior

In order to accomplish my dream, I expect myself to do the following:

1. _____
2. _____
3. _____
4. _____
5. _____

The Law of Self-Talk:

In order to accomplish my dream, I must have positive mental conversations with myself that say:

1. _____
2. _____
3. _____
4. _____
5. _____

*Now work your plan. It is all up to you!*

# **What do you make?**

*Choose to make a positive difference in the lives of others. Please remember that money and material things can feel good for a short time, but that will pass. Making a positive difference in another person's life can change the world.*

*We are all teachers of life. We are all role models. There are always people who look up to us and look to us for guidance and help. It could be a brother, sister, cousin, friend, or colleague. We also have people we look up to as well.*

*What do you make?*
*When looking at your future, please remember to make a difference—learn from and be a teacher of life.*

*Just as iron sharpens iron, people sharpen people.*

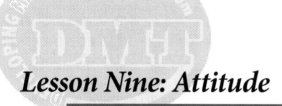

# Lesson Nine: Attitude

*Our attitude has a great impact on the level of success we will achieve in life.*
*Our attitude is how we look at the world and how the people of the world look back at us.*

Explanation:

Our attitude is our mental state. Our attitude is moldable. Our attitude is our choice. Only you can change your attitude. Our attitude can be influenced by many things. Our attitude is our outlook on the world.

Our attitude is either optimistic (positive) or pessimistic (negative). There is no in-between. Our attitudes will project what we want. A positive attitude is one that looks at the greatness in the world, sees the good in other people, and creates a happy, energetic, and up-beat person. A negative attitude is one that sees the bad in the world, sees the negative in other people, and creates a sad, mopey, and low-energy level person.

Ask yourself, "Would I want others to display my attitude? Is my attitude worth catching?" Remember, it is our attitude, not our aptitude (intelligence), that can determine our altitude. Our attitude is more important than our aptitude. When people ask you how you are, you can respond with "OK" or "I'm fantastic." Which response makes you feel better? The second response gives you more energy and makes people want to be around you. To have a neutral response like "OK" or even worse a negative response, steals energy from you and can turn your attitude into a negative one.

Examples of real-life applications:

Instructor: Give an example of how this lesson could apply to your life, family, or job.

How does your attitude apply to you?

How could you apply the attitude concept to a team or group?

How could you apply the attitude concept in school or on the job?

How could you apply the attitude concept at your home?

How could you apply the attitude concept to your life in the future?

# Lesson Ten: *Walking Between the Lines*

*Winning is not the most important thing; putting forth the effort to win is. The difference between whether we succeed or struggle is often in our attitude. To control your success, control the way you are looking at the world, and control your attitude.*

Explanation:

"Walking between the lines" means adapting our attitude and behavior to different environments. To help understand this better, we need to be aware that certain changes are expected of us when we are in different situations in our lives. Everybody acts differently in different environments. Understanding how we are supposed to act in those environments is critical to reaching our maximum potential.

Using our children and athletics for an example: We all want our kids to be nice, polite kids. But when athletes enter competition, we expect them to turn on a switch of desire, passion, mental toughness, self-discipline, self-confidence, and focus that will bring their games to the next level.

Understand this is no different than turning on the switch when we walk into any other environment. For example, when we walk into a church, think about how you're supposed to act. Now take that same switch and put yourself on the basketball floor, in a cross-country race, on a football field, soccer field, hockey arena, wrestling mat, or in any other competitive environment. Now think about how you're supposed to act. Let's use an extreme example: on the football field you are asked to be loud and tackle or block others. In church you are to keep quiet, listen, and not touch others. Let's say you tackled the priest as he was giving his sermon. How would tackling the priest be interpreted by others? Not good, I know. I understand that this is an extreme example, but the concept is the same. People who master this switch will have unlimited potential in his or her ability and life. This situation can be applied to band or choir, the classroom, home, or job, and many more of life's activities. As we get older, this applies to all areas of our lives. In athletics, it is known as "putting on your game face." In life, it is commonly referred to as "changing your hat."

Examples of real-life applications:

Instructor: Give an example of how this lesson could apply to your life, family, or job.

Project:

Do your parents act the same at work as they do at home? How are they different?

Do your coaches act the same when coaching as they do when they are not coaching? How are they different?

Does your principal act the same when he or she sees you in the halls versus if they have to see you in his or her office? How is he/she different?

Does your teacher act the same in the classroom as in other environments? How is he/she different?

Does an employers act the same at work as they do at home? How may they be different?

How does "walking between the lines" apply to you?

How could "walking between the lines" apply to a team or group?

How could you apply "walking between the lines" in school or on the job?

How could you apply "walking between the lines" at your home?

How could you apply "walking between the lines" to your life in the future?

# Lesson Eleven: An Attitude of Gratitude

*Showing gratitude is the simplest way to bring greatness to the world around you.*

Explanation:

Gratitude is simply appreciating the people and things around us and showing it. This is as simple as saying "thank you." It is easy to take things for granted. It is easy to get caught up in yourself. But remember, people never make it on their own. Other people give us the opportunity to achieve. There are literally hundreds of people who wait on you daily. They may get paid for it, or they may not. They all deserve to be appreciated. This takes very little time, effort, or thought, and it is very much appreciated by the people around us. Here's how it works:

"Dad, thank you for bringing me to practice today."

"Teacher X, thank you for teaching us about _____ today; I enjoyed that."

"Coach X, thanks for helping us with our offense today; I think I've got it."

"Janitor X, thank you for cleaning up after us each day; without you, we would have a pretty messy school."

"Principal X, thank you for keeping our school organized and on track. I appreciate you."

"Mom, thank you for going to work every day and providing us with the things we need to live the way we do."

A common quote for this is "Stopping to smell the roses." I like to say, "Stop and smell the roses—and thank the person who planted them."

Nobody has to do anything for anybody. If people know that we sincerely appreciate them, they will do more for us than you can possibly imagine. Think about the people around you, and recognize them. It is amazing how good it will make you feel to recognize others for the great things they do.

Project: Two Ways to Develop Gratitude:

1. Write three to five great things that happened to you today.

1._____

2._____

3._____

4._____

5._____

Note the great changes that occur in your life when focusing on positive things. Next, establish a "Gratitude Journal." Date it, and write down the positive things that happen to you on a daily basis. The best time to do this is before bed. This brings positive thoughts into your head, as opposed to thinking about your problems before bed. This will assist you in getting a night of restful sleep focused on attracting the positive to your life. Focus on the great things in your life, and great things will continue to happen to you!

2. Write a letter of gratitude. Write a letter telling someone that you appreciate all the great things that they do or have done for you or others. It is best to hand-deliver it, and then read it to the person you wrote it to. If you cannot do that, send it by mail or e-mail. It is gratifying to feel important in the lives of others. It is gratifying to tell others they are important in our lives. Showing our appreciation is a great way to spread good in the world. Letters of gratitude are one way to do this.

Acknowledging the good in the world will create more good for everyone. This is the Spiritual Law of Success.

Examples of real-life applications:

Instructor: Give an example of how this lesson could apply to your life, family, or job.

How does an attitude of gratitude apply to you?

How could an attitude of gratitude apply to a team or group?

How could you apply an attitude of gratitude in school or on the job?

How could you apply an attitude of gratitude at your home?

How could you apply an attitude of gratitude to your life in the future?

# Lesson Twelve: Failing Forward

*If we learn from defeat, we haven't really lost.*

Explanation:

When we look at failure, we first must understand what failure is *not*. Failure is *not*:

- Avoidable—we all will fail at times in our lives. Most of us will fail a lot more in some areas than others.
- An event—something doesn't just happen to us one day that makes us failures.
- Objective—yes, we can fail a test, but that doesn't make *us* failures.
- The enemy—failure is not a bad thing. It helps us see what does not work, so we can make a change and see what will work.
- Irreversible—oftentimes, when we make a mistake or do not get the result we had hoped for, we can change what we did and anticipate a different result. To do the *same thing* and expect a different result could be considered a form of insanity.
- A stigma—failure does not just follow us around, but we *can* attract it by negative thinking.
- Final—when we fail, it does not make us failures, or failures for the rest of our lives.

It has been estimated that Thomas Edison failed ten thousand times before he invented the light bulb. When asked why he kept trying after so many failures, he said he didn't fail ten thousand times; he just found out what would not work ten thousand times. Thomas Edison also invented many other things while on his quest to invent the light bulb. He found many other opportunities along his way that he later took advantage of.

In order to succeed, we must fail. Just make sure you *fail forward*. Failure is the price we pay to achieve success. Learn from your successful failures.

To understand achievers, realized that they:

- Reject rejection
- See failure as temporary
- See failure as an isolated incident
- Focus on strengths
- Vary approaches to achieving
- Bounce back
- Don't blame
- Put failures into perspective and change it into a step toward success

Achievers achieve!

Are you riding down the "Failure Freeway?"

- Do you get angry often? Especially over little things?
- Do you try to cover things up instead of taking responsibility for your actions?
- Do you see yourself speeding up, going faster and faster down this path of doom until you finally feel like …
- Giving up?

If you *are* riding down "Failure Freeway," wake up and find an exit!

If you always do what you have always done, you will always receive what you have always received. All successful people take responsibility for themselves and live by their own character.

*According to Michael Jordan, "I have missed thousands of shots and lost hundreds of games. I was entrusted with taking the winning shot multiple times—and missed. I failed over and over again, and that is exactly why I succeed."*
*Michael Jordan learned to fail forward.*

Examples of real-life applications:

Instructor: Give an example of how this lesson could apply to your life, family, or job.

How could failing forward apply to you?

How could failing forward apply to a team or group?

How could you apply failing forward in school or on the job?

How could you apply failing forward at your home?

How could you apply failing forward to your life in the future?

*Just as a kite rises against the wind, do not be afraid of resistance.*
*Refuse to join if things go wrong.*
*There is no such thing as failure—just feedback.*

# Lesson Thirteen: Perseverance

Explanation:

Perseverance is the ability to continue your efforts in spite of opposition or resistance. Perseverance is to fulfill your dream, and not allow other people or things to get in the way. Understand that you can be smart, know many people, and be very lucky—but hard work is the common thread in all successful people. Perseverance is all the hard work that we do, after all the hard work we have done.

Those who tried, even when it felt hopeless, have achieved many great things. When the going gets tough, the tough get focused, plan, execute, and achieve. Success is achieved by those who try and keep trying.

Examples of real-life applications:

Instructor: Give an example of how this lesson could apply to your life, family, or job.

How does perseverance apply to you?

How could perseverance apply to a team or group?

How could you apply perseverance in school or on the job?

How could you apply perseverance at your home?

How could you apply perseverance to your life in the future?

*If it weren't for obstacles, we would really never know whether we truly want something or just
think we do. Obstacles are there to show how much we really want it.
It is better to move slowly forward than to take one step backwards.*

# Lesson Fourteen: Understanding Human Development

Explanation:

During the first ten years of our lives, we think our parents know everything. They are the smartest people in the world. During this stage, we are impressed with our parents. We may even want to marry one of them.

As we mature, around eleven to fifteen years of age, we enter what I call the "why" stage. This is when we start wondering or asking why our parents, friends, or relatives do certain things that do not make sense to us:

- Why does he talk to me that way?
- Why does she treat me that way?
- Why does he always speed when he drives?
- Why do I have to be home at midnight?
- Why do I have to mow the yard?
- Why do I have to stack the firewood?
- Why do I have to shovel the walk?
- Why does she always ask me about my grades?
- Why does he always ask me about my practice?
- Why, why, why …

As we develop, around sixteen to twenty-one years of age, we enter what I call the "I can do better than they can," or "they are stupid" stage of our development. This is a difficult stage for parents and teenagers. The parents draw on life experiences to establish rules for the household; the teenagers want to flex their I-am-growing-up muscles. The teenagers question many things their parents (or others in authority) tell them. They feel they can do better than their parents, and they are going to prove it to them.

This is the tipping point in the long-term relationship of these individuals. Teenagers and parents must handle this correctly, or the long-term relationship may be tarnished for many years. Teenagers must look to their own integrity. If they can see that the person in authority (parent, coach, or other) is trying to protect them or position them to have fewer problems, then the teenagers must trust the authority's judgment. If teenagers choose not to follow this judgment and they get "caught," then they have to suffer the consequences of their actions. Parents and others in authority may let teenagers make their own mistakes so they can learn by their experience. This is a difficult task for both sides. The teenagers think they know what is best, and the parents don't want the teenagers to make the same mistakes they may have made. We must go through this process to develop a great future relationship.

After age twenty-one, we many times will look back at our lives and think to ourselves, "They were not so stupid after all." If we make it through the above stages with respect for each other, we will have wonderful, long-term relationships with the people we care about.

It is important to understand that we must go through these stages to develop a strong, long-term relationship. We will go through this process in all meaningful human relationships: parent-child, boyfriend-girlfriend, coach-player, husband-wife, and employer-employee. In some instances, it will take years to go through this process (parent-child), and in others it may take just weeks (employer-employee). The important thing to understand is that we must go through *all* of these stages to have a quality, long-term relationship.

The people who have problems working through these stages may end up with multiple divorces and have difficulty holding jobs. They may never reach the level of success they may dream of because they pull the plug and move in a different direction too quickly. Remember, it is necessary to go through this process to succeed.

Understanding this process early in life will help us understand where we are in human relationship development when we feel frustration with future relationships. This is okay and is normal to go through if we want something to work out for the long term. When you are feeling these emotions, ask yourself, "Where am I at in my development in this relationship? Do I want this relationship to last?" If the relationship is not important, pull the plug. If it is important to have the relationship last, control your thoughts, actions, and feelings, and continue down the road toward a successful relationship.

Understanding human relationships will assist us in determining where we are going and what lies ahead in many relationships. By understanding the basic concepts of developing human relationships, we will avoid pitfalls in relationships. We will have less frustration and greater confidence with the development or termination of future relationships.

Examples of real-life applications:

Instructor: Give an example of how this lesson could apply to your life, family, or job.

How does understanding human relationships apply to you?

How could understanding human relationships apply to a team or group?

How could you apply your understanding of human relationships in school or on the job?

How could you apply your understanding of human relationships at your home?

How could you apply your understanding of human relationships to your life in the future?

# A Red Flag in Human Relationships

There is a *red flag* in human relationships. This is the rare occasion when one person may take advantage of a situation and attempt to lead another person down the wrong path. This can happen with any two people. For this example lets use an adult (coach) and a teenager (player). This usually begins with the adult befriending the teenager. The adult may do things for the teenager; spend time with them, buy things for them, compliment them, help them with projects, take then fishing, etc. The adult gains the trust and respect of the teenager. After the adult has gained the teenager's trust and respect, the adult belittles, degrades, and intimidates the teenager. The adult may feel this will make the teenager stronger or will "toughen him up". Many times it does not, it can actually crush the teenager's self-esteem causing him to doubt himself. Be careful of these bullying tactics. Recognize this as a manipulation and intimidation tactic that can be bad for the teenager's future development. Continuing to be involved with this type of relationship can negatively affect our lives—if we choose to allow them to.

This is not a healthy situation. This type of relationship needs to be addressed and changed or terminated. When a teenager (or the teenager's parent) addresses this situation, be prepared for manipulation and guilt tactics from the adult. One of the most common ones is an avoidance behavior, treating you like you are invisible or do not exist. Going from your "best friend" to "you do not exist". This can be confusing for the teenager. This can make the teenager (or the teenager's parent) feel guilty or feel like they did something wrong. This is the adult's weakness and is a last effort "guilt tactic" to get the teenager back on their side. The adult may even go as far as to recruit other adults to think the teenager (or parent) has done something wrong. The other adults may also not communicate with the teenager (or parent). Do not fall for these or any other manipulation tactics. Do what is best for you. It is the teenager's choice to stop this behavior. It may be difficult, but do not be manipulated by others' bullying tactics.

Those who choose to use these bullying tactics are usually emotionally weak and insecure with themselves but appear to be very confident. Remember, our path in life is established by our morals, ethics, values and choices. You establish your life. If your values (whatever you choose your values to be) are being violated by anyone, you need to address it. Fix it, or terminate the relationship. Do not get trapped in an unhealthy relationship with anyone.

It is unfortunate, but some teachers, coaches, employers, and people in general take this approach in building relationships, either knowingly or unknowingly. It is important that we recognize this, identify it as unacceptable behavior, and resolve the situation by fixing or terminating the relationship. You are in control of your destiny. Your life is your choice. *Do not be manipulated by others.*

# Lesson Fifteen: Being Teachable

*Wise people learn from the experience of others.*
*Watch others, see their successes and failures, apply them to yourself, and achieve success.*

Explanation:

Being teachable means having the ability to be taught. It is the ability to listen and apply what is being taught. Ask questions if needed, but *don't* talk back or be disrespectful. This type of attitude will only hurt the relationship. This is a lose-lose situation. Do things the way you are taught, not your way. When being taught, exercise good communication techniques, as taught in this book, maintaining good eye contact. Being teachable is having the desire to listen and willingly make the changes that others are requesting.

Hint: When a person is making recommendations for change, *teaching you*, it is not a personal attack on you. It is an attempt to put you in a better position to succeed. Some instructors (especially coaches, band instructors and some employers and teachers) can have loud, harsh voices. Do yourself a favor: listen to *what* they are saying, not *how* they are saying it. When a person has passion for what they are trying to teach, emotions can run rampant, especially in sporting events. Apply what they tell you as well as you can. Using a coaching example: When a coach is coaching you up on the bench or sideline, look him or her directly in the eyes, understand the information, and then say something like this: "Coach, I understand that you want me to … Is that correct?" If the coach says yes, continue making direct eye contact and say, "I got it; I'll get the job done," or, "I will do better next time." My guess is that the coach will put you right back in the game to let you prove yourself. Being teachable is the ability to listen, learn, and apply what you have been taught. Being teachable will be used many times in your life.

From the standpoint of a teacher, parent, coach, or employer, (being the teacher) it is important to be an excellent communicator. Be aware of the words you choose to use. Two things can never be recovered: time after it is gone and a word after it is spoken. Attempt to have a calm,

confident, compassionate tone to your voice. Attempt to have positive body language and facial expressions. Doing these simple things will encourage others to perform their best. If we choose to acknowledge the positive (and correct the negative), we will get more positive results. Make a big deal out of the great things that others do, and you will help to create great people.

Examples of real-life applications:

Instructor: Give an example of how this lesson could apply to your life, family, or job.

How does being teachable apply to you?

How could being teachable apply to a team or group?

How could you apply being teachable in school or on the job?

How could you apply being teachable at your home?

How could you apply being teachable to your life in the future?

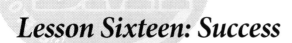

# Lesson Sixteen: Success

*Success is the gradual accomplishment of our dreams or goals.*

Explanation:

Success is the achievement of something intended or desired. Success is the gradual realization of a thought or idea. There are many definitions of success. Your success should only be defined by you. Success is achieved by reaching our optimum potential, by achieving our personal goals and dreams.

Success is something you attract by the person you become. Your success is developed by working on *you*, not by changing others. Once we realize this, we will know what to work on. To earn, buy, or win something is a minor thing; to *become* something is a major thing. Once we realize this, our lives will explode into change!

You are the only one who can determine your success or lack thereof. Success is achieved by those who try and keep trying. All people want to succeed. Some people want to succeed so badly that they are willing to work for it. None of the success secrets will work unless *you* work.

Maintaining long-term success can be difficult for some. Sometimes it is harder to be a success than to become a success. Too many times, people destroy their own success. After you have achieved success, remember: honesty and humility are the keys to maintaining long-term success.

You have every characteristic you need to succeed. As Nike says, "Just do it!"

Examples of real-life applications:

Instructor: Give an example of how this lesson could apply to your life, family, or job.

How does the lesson of success apply to you?

How could the lesson of success apply to a team or group?

How could you apply the lesson of success in school or on the job?

How could you apply the lesson of success at your home?

How could you apply the lesson of success to your life in the future?

*The higher we go,*
*the farther we can see,*
*the less crowded it is, and*
*the easier it is for others to take shots at us.*

*Do not let others destroy your feelings of success.*
*Their jealousy is their weakness, not yours.*
*Be proud of your accomplishments, no matter how big or how small.*
*Your accomplishments are your successes.*
*You have earned them and deserve them.*
*Enjoy them!*

# *Lesson Seventeen: Integrity*

*What lies behind us and what lies before us are tiny matters compared to what lies within us.*

*—Ralph Waldo Emerson*

Explanation

Integrity is the ability to maintain "moral soundness." Moral soundness means the ability to determine right from wrong and make the correct choice.

Integrity is doing the right thing even when no one is watching. Integrity is doing the right thing even when it is difficult, even if you have to stand-alone for the right reasons.

There are many ways to describe integrity: truthfulness, truth-seeking, striving for excellence, and diligence are a few.

Examples of real-life applications:

Instructor: Give an example of how this lesson could apply to your life, family, or job.

How does integrity apply to you?

How could integrity apply to a team or group?

How could you apply integrity in school or on the job?

How could you apply integrity at your home?

How could you apply integrity to your life in the future?

*What lies within you?*
*What do you expect of yourself?*

# Lesson Eighteen: Respect

Explanation:

Respect is the special consideration that you hold for yourself or for another person or thing. If you want the respect of others, show respect to yourself and others. The concept of respect is very broad in nature and can be used in almost all aspects of life. The following are some examples of respect:

- Being polite; using please and thank you
- Looking a person squarely in the eyes when you are communicating
- Looking interested when a person is speaking to you
- Taking your shoes off at the door when visiting another person's home
- Calling people "Mr." or "Mrs."
- Not littering

Respect is a habit that will take us far if we choose to use it. *Disrespect* will hold us back like an anchor dragging behind a ship.

It is important to have respect for other people and other things, but it is most important to respect yourself.

Examples of real-life applications:

Instructor: Give an example of how this lesson could apply to your life, family, or job.

How does respect apply to you?

How could respect apply to a team or group?

How could you apply respect in school or on the job?

How could you apply respect at your home?

How could you apply respect to your life in the future?

# *Lesson Nineteen: Humility*

Explanation:

Humility is the state of being humble. Being humble means not getting too caught up in our accomplishments, not getting a big head, and not being arrogant. Humility has some specific traits: being able to apologize, being able to listen, being grateful, and forgiving without holding a grudge. This has been called being "transparent." This means people can see who you are. Their first impression is usually the right impression. Humility is the ability to enjoy the good things that happen to you with the people who helped you achieve them.

Examples of real-life applications:

Instructor: Give an example of how this lesson could apply to your life, family, or job.

How does humility apply to you?

How could humility apply to a team or group?

How could you apply humility in school or on the job?

How could you apply humility at your home?

How could you apply humility to your life in the future?

# Lesson Twenty: Developing Successful Team Dynamics

*Footnote: The values model or framework discussed in this chapter is taken from the work of Richard M. Biery, M.D. as presented in the white paper titled "The Virtue-Based Value Model for Organizational Behavior".*

A team is an interesting concept. Some people do not have the characteristics that enable them to work in a team setting; therefore, they may be more successful in individual activities. Developing team dynamics can be a difficult task. One way is to educate a team on what types of *values* are required to develop successful team dynamics. Some *individual values* are critical to the development of a successful team. These are the values we look for when finding a quality teammate: integrity, respect and humility. I call these values the three prongs of the "Team Triangle." Integrity consists of truthfulness, truth-seeking, excellence, and diligence. Respect consists of thoughtfulness, devotion, loyal caring, cooperation, and positive human relationships. Humility consists of being able to apologize, being able to listen, being grateful, and being able to forgive without holding a grudge. Having these three characteristics (integrity, respect, and humility) has been called being transparent. In this context, transparent means "you see what you get." In the middle of the triangle, holding it all together, is one word: *courage*—the courage to make the right decisions at the right times for the right reasons. Even when the right decision is the hard decision.

## Team Triangles

Individual Values

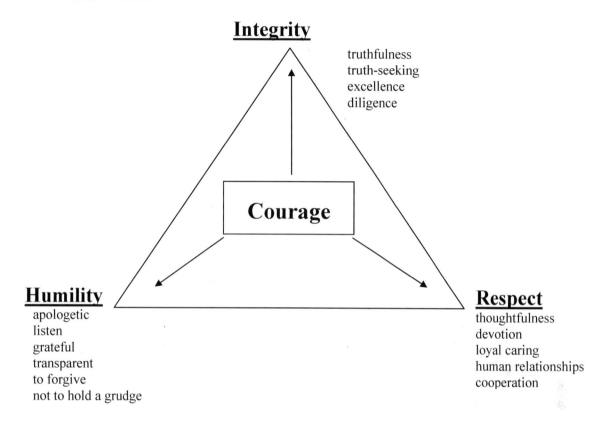

**Integrity**

truthfulness
truth-seeking
excellence
diligence

**Courage**

**Humility**
apologetic
listen
grateful
transparent
to forgive
not to hold a grudge

**Respect**
thoughtfulness
devotion
loyal caring
human relationships
cooperation

Ask yourself this question: Would you want a teammate who possesses the individual values of integrity, respect, and humility? If your answer is yes, then others expect the same for you. Do you possess these values?

In order to attain a successful team, the players must possess quality team values. Each person must possess the individual values of integrity, respect, and humility. Once these individual values are established, the individual can start to be a good teammate. You have begun to develop quality team values. This will also develop strong, successful team dynamics. To build quality team values, players must have mastered individual values. Having integrity and respect builds the team value of trust or trustworthiness. Having respect and humility develops the team value of unselfishness. Unselfishness is not limited to just material things. Unselfishness is sharing, being generous, giving of self, giving of recognition, and being open. Having humility and integrity builds the team values of a *restrained ego,* or the ability to be humble. Humility and integrity also assist in making us teachable.

Team Values

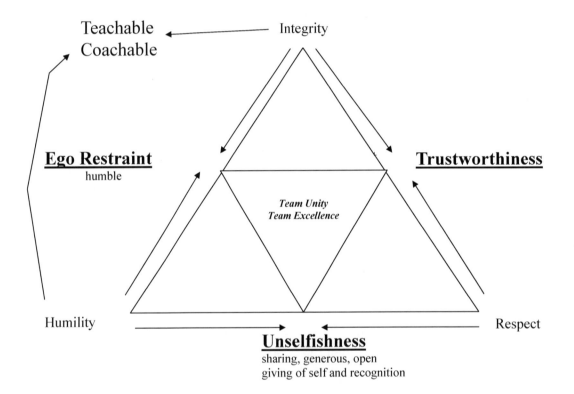

By possessing the individual values of integrity, respect, and humility, a team can build ego restraint, trust, and unselfishness. Integrity and humility are key components to being coached or taught. These team values build team unity, which results in a great team. The opportunity here is that these are all learned traits. This means these traits are teachable and learnable. These traits can be developed to build a great team.

A team is the bringing together of people with different backgrounds, morals, ethics, and life experiences for the purpose of achieving a goal. Because of all the variables involved in a team, half of the battle is getting that team to work together. Too often, teams play as a group of individuals. When a team plays as a group of individuals, players are usually more focused on their own performances than the performance of the team. This is the group of individuals who would rather hit three home runs and lose the game than go hitless and win. It is important to keep track of statistics for both individuals and teams, but never put individual statistics ahead of team statistics.

On most teams, there is a group of more talented athletes and a group of less talented athletes. It is important to remember that all athletes will have an opportunity to succeed based on what they contribute to the team. Some teammates' only job may be to participate in practice. This is that individual's contribution to the team success. Some teammates may be in the spotlight more than others. Understand that this is part of the game: you cannot have a team without all of the players. A team has reached true success when all players can celebrate the individual successes and sacrifices each player contributed to create the success of the team.

*"Every dog has his day."* The true measure of a successful team is when everyone feels great about the individual accomplishments that achieve the team goals.

Teamwork:
*Coming together is a beginning*
*Staying together is a process*
*Working together is success*

These team concepts will be used every day of your life in your family, education, and career. Mastering the ability to be a great teammate will prepare us for life now and in the future.

Examples of real-life applications:

Instructor: Give an example of how this lesson could apply to your life, family, or job.

How does the team concept apply to you?

How could the team concept apply to a team or group?

How could you apply the team concept in school or on the job?

How could you apply the team concept at your home?

How could you apply the team concept to your life in the future?

*"Sticks in a bundle are unbreakable."*
*—Kenyan proverb*

# Lesson Twenty-one: Being Competitive

*It is not the size of the dog in the fight; it is the size of the fight in the dog.*
*The greater the dream, the greater the obstacles, the greater the rewards.*

Explanation:

There are some basic components to becoming competitive in sports and competitive in life.

In sports you need to understand:

- The skills of the sport
- The fundamentals of the sport
- Passion and motivation—getting yourself and your team fired up and ready for practice, training, or an event
- Desire—applying what you learn, working hard, and building a team by complimenting others and noticing their good points
- Mental toughness—believing in yourself and your team no matter what the circumstances.

As athletes get older and more involved in sports, they begin to even out. Some are a little taller, a little quicker, a little more coordinated. Young people mature at different rates, but, all in all, most even out by about the ninth grade. So the question is: What separates good athletes from great athletes?

The answer? *Desire, passion, self-discipline, and mental toughness:* the desire to master and apply the skills and fundamentals of the sports you are in; the passion to motivate yourself and your team to accomplish outlandish goals; the self-discipline and mental toughness to play as hard as you can every second you are at a practice or in a game.

Skills and fundamentals are taught and drilled. You will continue to be taught and drilled on fundamentals throughout your life.

Becoming passionate, showing desire, being self-disciplined, and demonstrating mental toughness are learned behaviors are also contagious traits. Unfortunately, so is their lack!

Such is life. These characteristics come from within you. You need to become self-disciplined to accomplish your life's dreams. We need to have the desire to make ourselves better at all that we do. We need to have the passion to motivate ourselves and our team, no matter if you're happy or sad, sick or healthy. We need mental toughness to believe in ourselves and our team no matter what happens. Life is competitive. Learning to compete early in life will prepare us for the competitions of the future.

Examples of real-life applications:

Instructor: Give an example of how this lesson could apply to your life, family, or job.

How does being competitive apply to you?

How could being competitive apply to a team or group?

How could you apply being competitive in school or on the job?

How could you apply being competitive at your home?

How could you apply being competitive to your life in the future?

# Lesson Twenty-two: Playing to the Level of Your Competition

*Much of our success or failure is determined by our will to win.*

Explanation:

Playing to the level of our competition can be a common problem in athletics and in life. In life, a common cliché is, "Keeping up with the neighbors." In athletics, this is demonstrated when playing an inferior team. A team with more talent may (consciously or unconsciously) think they are going to win. They may play with less discipline, playing down to the level of their competition. This can put the talented team in a position to lose the game. A team may also play another team that is much more talented than they are. This can encourage the weaker team to be more focused and play with much more discipline, resulting in an upset.

I am finding that more people are playing to the level of their competition. This may be developed in our backyards, where older, more talented friends or siblings are taught to let the younger, less talented child win. This is the "nice guy" approach. This approach is okay, but please understand there is a time and a place. It is okay in the backyard. But in an organized competition that is important to you, you must bring your best every time. This is "walking between the lines." It is putting on your game face and maintaining it for the entire competition. To give up (consciously or unconsciously) and play to the level of your competition is the easy thing to do. To maintain the level of your game and play to your potential is difficult, but it is a must for success. This is a learned behavior, and it must be reinforced at every practice and game. Remember—when it matters, never lower your standards. Playing to the level of your competition can easily transfer over to schoolwork, a job, or your relationships with your family. Always work your hardest, and you will always have success. This is life. Set your expectations high and attain them. It does not matter what others have or do. Remember that your life is up to you, not to others.

Examples of real-life applications:

Instructor: Give an example of how this lesson could apply to your life, family, or job.

How does "Playing to the Level of Your Competition" apply to you?

How could "Playing to the Level of Your Competition" apply to a team or group?

How could you apply "Playing to the Level of Your Competition" in school or on the job?

How could you apply "Playing to the Level of Your Competition" at your home?

How could you apply "Playing to the Level of Your Competition" to your life in the future?

# Lesson Twenty-three: Leadership

*Leadership is doing the right things for the right reasons, even when nobody is watching.*

Explanation:

Many people think that leadership at a young age is inherent. It is my opinion that leadership is a learned behavior. Some have stated that leadership is actually the ability to help others. I think that leadership has many facets, including helpfulness, honesty, integrity, perseverance, and self-control. This could also be called an indomitable spirit.

Leadership is built on morals and ethics. With good morals and ethics, you can lead people effectively toward success. If you don't have good morals and ethics, you cannot effectively lead others. Many people want to be led; the question is, where are they being led? Are they being led down the road of success, or are they being led to adversity?

A leader must possess a set of distinctive traits I like to call the six C's:

Courage
Competence
Candor
Commitment
Compassion
Communication

In order to follow a leader down the road of success, people need to understand that their leader has these distinctive traits:

1. Courage: This means moving forward in spite of difficult circumstances.

2. Competence: People need to believe their leader is smart enough or qualified enough to lead them.

3. Candor: This is being sincere and frank—a leader must speak from the heart.

4. Commitment: People must trust their leader to follow through to the end.

5. Compassion: This means caring about others in good times and bad; it means to help celebrate the good and offer counsel for the bad.

6. Communication: This is the ability to convey information in a clear, concise, consistent and courteous way, encouraging others to apply what is being communicated.

Strong leaders use the six C's to accomplish what needs to be accomplished. From these six C's, followers develop confidence and trust in their leadership.

Understanding Leadership:

As a leader, we will win some and lose some. Win more than you lose, and you're winning the game.

The number of people who follow us will vary. As we improve as a leader more will follow. If we develop poor leadership traits, less may follow. Remember, some will follow; some will not. We cannot lead those who do not want to be lead. As we get better at leading, more will follow.

There are times when things do not work at all. Take the risk; make modifications and try it again—or stop it and move on, learning from your experience.

Great leaders can see things that do not exist.

Great leaders can dream big dreams.

Great leaders have faith in themselves and the people around them.

Great leaders have distinctive leadership traits. Great leaders:

- have candor, but are not rude
- have compassion, but are not weak
- are thoughtful, but not lazy

- have courage, but are not bullies
- are humble, but not timid
- have commitment, but not tunnel vision
- are competent, but not arrogant
- are humorous, but not silly
- communicate *with*, not *at* others
- dream great dreams
- lead with great purpose

Leadership Project

Please read the information below. You don't have to actually answer the questions. Just read it straight through, and you'll get the point.

Name the three wealthiest people in the world.

Name the last three Super Bowl winners.

Name the last three Heisman Trophy winners.

Name the last three winners of the Miss America pageant.

Name three people who have won the Nobel or Pulitzer Prize.

Name the last three Academy Award winners for best actor and actress.

Name the last three World Series winners.

How did you do?

The point is, most of us do not remember many of the people in the past, even if they were the best in their field.

Here's another quiz.

List three teachers who eased your journey through school.

Name three friends who have helped you through a difficult time.

Name three people who have taught you something worthwhile.

Think of three people who have made you feel appreciated and special.

Think of three people you enjoy spending time with.

Easier?

The lesson: The people who make a difference in our lives are not the ones with the most credentials, the most money, or the most awards. They are the ones who care. In order to make a difference in others, great leaders *care*.

Examples of real-life applications:

Instructor: Give an example of how this lesson could apply to your life, family, or job.

How does the lesson of leadership apply to you?

How could the lesson of leadership apply to a team or group?

How could you apply the lesson of leadership in school or on the job?

How could you apply the lesson of leadership at your home?

How could you apply the lesson of leadership to your life in the future?

# Lesson Twenty-four: Communication

*Communication is the single most important aspect of leadership.*

Explanation:

Communication means to give or pass on information; it means to have others understand your ideas.

There are many forms of communication. The two most important are:

- Verbal (talking)
- Nonverbal (body language and facial expressions)

Understanding the "communication loop": The communication loop consists of giving information, receiving and comprehending the information, and then applying what was communicated. If the communication loop is not completed, then there are loose ends. If there are loose ends, then *miscommunication* has occurred, and frustration builds in both the giver and the receiver of the information. To form the communication loop, two things must occur.

1. Information must be provided.

2. An acknowledgment that the information was received and understood must be given.

If the acknowledgment that the information was received and understood is *not* communicated back to the information provider, it is *normal* human behavior for the provider to become louder, more direct, and less compassionate. This can turn into yelling! The communication loop is critical in all relationships.

Communication Project:

It is very important to have as many people as you can role-play in this lesson.

Demonstrate verbal communication skills. Give examples of words, tone, and volume differences that can change the context of the communication delivered. How we deliver information is as important as what we say. When giving information, try to be loud with compliments and quiet with corrections. When receiving information, attempt to listen to *what* the giver is saying, and not *how* she or he is saying it. In regard to coaching, coaching can be an emotional roller coaster. Sometimes coaches and athletes get loud when they are trying to get a point across. This is not personal; rather, it can be part of the emotion of the game. Unfortunately, it can be perceived as quite negative by many that witness it.

Understanding verbal communication:

- Explain and demonstrate negative words, tone (especially sarcasm), and volume.
- Explain and demonstrate positive words, tone (especially sincerity), and volume.

After receiving information, close the communication loop by saying, "I understand." Better yet, repeat what was communicated to you to confirm that you received it correctly from the giver. Then say, "I can do that!" Then do it.

Understanding body language (non-verbal communication):

Negative:

Explain and demonstrate not paying attention by looking around, shaking your head, slouching, looking away, and crossing your arms. Include negative facial expressions such as grimacing, frowning, and closing or rolling your eyes.

Positive:

Explain and demonstrate paying attention, including leaning forward and making

eye contact. Demonstrate nodding your head and a look of concentration.

Communication is a two-way street—giving it and receiving it. *How the information is given and how it is received is as important as the interpretation of the information itself.*

Information + how information is given + how information is received = *communication.*

Examples of real-life applications:

Instructor: Give an example of how this lesson could apply to your life, family, or job.

How does the lesson of communication apply to you?

How could the lesson of communication apply to a team or group?

How could you apply the lesson of communication in school or on the job?

How could you apply the lesson of communication at your home?

How could you apply the lesson of communication to your life in the future?

# Lesson Twenty-five: The Art of Meeting Another Person

*First impressions last a lifetime!*
*A good, firm handshake is a positive step to a long lasting first impression.*

Explanation:

There is only one chance to make a first impression. The way you meet others influences their opinions of you. It is important that you learn how to meet other people in a confident and respectful manner.

To give a good first impression:

- Look the other person directly in the eye.
- Smile.
- Introduce yourself by your full name. "Hello, Jon. My name is Bob Smith. It is a pleasure to meet you." Or, "It is nice to meet you."
- Extend a firm handshake.
- Pay the person a compliment, such as, "I've heard nice things about you."
- Ask questions about the other person. "Where are you from? What do you do for fun? Do you enjoy sports?"
- At the end of the conversation, bow out gracefully by making eye contact and saying something like, "It was great meeting you, Jon or Mr. _____." Use the person's name, give a firm handshake, smile, and say, "Have a great day."

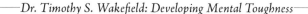

This will make a positive, long-lasting impression on the people you meet. A first impression is one of the things people most remember about you.

Examples of real-life applications:

Instructor: Give an example of how this lesson could apply to your life, family, or job.

Role-Playing:

Explain and demonstrate "The Art of Meeting Another Person." This is something that many people feel is taught at home, but in reality, it is not. Take time to be very thorough in this area. It will make a lasting impression on young people. This is something they will use for the rest of their lives, and it will take practice to master. This can give them great confidence when interacting with their peers, and it may assist them in future interviews.

How does "The Art of Meeting Another Person" apply to you?

How could "The Art of Meeting Another Person" apply to a team or group?

How could you apply "The Art of Meeting Another Person" in school or on the job?

How could you apply "The Art of Meeting Another Person" at your home?

How could you apply "The Art of Meeting Another Person" to your life in the future?

# My Hope For You

- *I hope you have been spanked on the butt for something you did wrong and padded on the back for something you did right.*
- *I hope you learn trust by being betrayed and learn to trust yourself and others.*
- *I hope you learn to forgive others and forgive yourself.*
- *I hope you have learned the importance of reading, writing, and doing math.*
- *I hope you learn and never tire of learning.*
- *I hope you have swore and learned what soap tastes like.*
- *I hope you see an animal born and an animal die and be aware of your emotions with both.*
- *I hope you make time for your children, brothers, sisters, parents, grandparents, aunts, and uncles. In the end they may be all you have.*
- *I hope you kiss your mother and hug your father often.*
- *I hope you fight for something you believe in and feel disappointment if you lose and feel honor if you win.*
- *If you choose to consume alcohol, remember to control it and not have it control you.*
- *I hope you never smoke or suffer its effects.*
- *I hope you never use illegal drugs or hang out with the people who do.*
- *I hope you stub your toe, twist your ankle, skin your shin, and burn your finger.*
- *I hope you learn to dig in the dirt, plant a garden, and eat what it produces.*
- *I hope you plant a tree and come back twenty years later to see what you gave the opportunity to grow.*
- *I hope you have been teased about someone you like.*
- *I hope you are cheated, so you learn to be honest.*
- *I hope you are humiliated, so you learn to be humble.*
- *I hope someone is rude to you, so you learn to be polite and kind.*
- *If you tell a lie I hope you get caught and feel what it is like to confess.*
- *If you steal I hope you are caught and pay your consequences.*
- *I hope you learn to feel good about yourself and others.*
- *I hope you learn to recognize the positive in others, tell them, and the people that care about them.*
- *I hope you learn to keep your mouth shut when you see the negative in others.*
- *I hope you learn to: Wash your dishes, stack firewood, mow your yard, change your oil, build a fire, wash your clothes, make your food, and clean your house.*
- *I hope you learn to laugh at yourself and not at others.*
- *I hope you learn to laugh loud and laugh often.*
- *I hope you learn happiness comes from within not from having more.*
- *I hope you learn life is not fair, no one can do it for you and you have no one to blame but yourself.*
- *I hope you learn to say I love you and mean it.*
- *I hope you learn to love yourself and others.*
- *I hope you take chances, fail and succeed.*
- *I hope you learn to help those that want to be helped not those that need to be helped.*
- *I hope you learn to be a servant to many.*
- *I hope you learn to pray. Respecting a higher power, asking forgiveness, showing appreciation for all of your gifts, praying to help others, and praying to help yourself.*
- *My hope for you is: Hard work, disappointment, pain, forgiveness, trust, self-dependence, honor, pride, respect, self-discipline, dignity, laughter, happiness, love, failure, success, to serve, and to respect a higher power. These things are what bring out the best in life.*

# Lesson Twenty-six: Mastering the Things That Don't Take Talent

*Some people make things happen, some people watch things happen, and some people wonder what happened. Be proactive—make a difference in your life by mastering the things that do not take talent.*

Explanation:

To catapult you toward success in life, it is important first to master the things that do not take talent. Then you can advance with the talents you are given. The things that do not take talent are called the fundamentals—of a sport, or of life.

Example in athletics:

Does it take talent to hustle in any sport?
In basketball, does it take talent to box out?
In football, does it take talent to know the play or be in the right stance?
In baseball, does it take talent to watch the ball hit your bat or put your glove on the ground?

These are fundamentals. These are things that must be mastered. Once you can master these things, you can let your talents move you to the next level of achievement.

Examples in life:

Does it take any talent to be polite? To say please and thank you?
Does it take any talent to be on time for school or work?
Does it take any talent to let others know you appreciate them?
Does it take any talent to see a piece of litter on the ground, pick it up, and throw it away?

These things don't take talent. These things take discipline, and the ability to master these things will catapult you ahead in life.

An athlete can overcome a lack of talent by mastering the things that don't require talent. A lesser athlete can pass up a gifted athlete by mastering the things that do not require talent (if the gifted athlete does not).

Project:

In this project, we will identify a sport/activity you're involved in (write the name of the sport or activity on the line), your school/job, and your home. Next, identify five things in each area that do not require talent.

| Sport/ activity:_____ | School/job: | Your home: |
|---|---|---|
| 1. | 1. | 1. |
| 2. | 2. | 2. |
| 3. | 3. | 3. |
| 4. | 4. | 4. |
| 5. | 5. | 5. |

Now, at every practice, game, or exposure, work on these and make yourself better.

Next, identify five things in your life that do not require talent.

1._____

2._____

3._____

4._____

5._____

By identifying things that do not take talent to perform, you can make yourself better at life.

Examples of real-life applications:

Instructor: Give an example of how this lesson could apply to your life, family, or job.

How does mastering the things that don't take talent apply to you?

How could mastering the things that don't take talent apply to a team or group?

How could you apply mastering the things that don't take talent in school or on the job?

How could you apply mastering the things that don't take talent at your home?

How could you apply mastering the things that don't take talent to your life in the future?

# Lesson Twenty-Seven: Refusing to Lose

*What you receive from reaching your goal is not nearly as important as what you become by reaching your goal.*
*Attributed to Zig Ziglar*

Explanation:

It is not the best team that wins; it is the team that refuses to lose. This is simply *desire*.

The definition of desire is: *to want!* Desire is to want to have, acquire, or bring something about; it is to want to make a change in order to succeed; it is to have the desire to make yourself the best you can be; desire is to view sacrifices as the building blocks of your future.

Have the desire to make a change when someone is explaining something to you. Have the desire to work on your skills. Have the desire to understand you will not do things perfectly the first time and many times thereafter. Have the desire to be teachable so you and the people around you can be your best.

This is a conscious decision to be the best you can be. Having a burning internal desire is the fuel of passion and the will to win. Desire creates power. Desire is the great equalizer.

Examples of real-life applications:

Instructor: Give an example of how this lesson could apply to your life, family, or job.

How does refusing to lose apply to you?

How could refusing to lose apply to a team or group?

How could you apply refusing to lose in school or on the job?

How could you apply refusing to lose at your home?

How could you apply refusing to lose to your life in the future?

# *Lesson Twenty-eight: Expanding Your Quitting Point*

*Opportunity lies within us and not within the job.*
*The job is the mirror of each of us.*

Explanation:

It is important to understand that everybody has a quitting point. Some people quit sooner than others, and many times they have less success. Other people are able to expand their quitting points—some will almost physically break down before they quit. By pushing yourself to your quitting point, you will expand your quitting point physically and mentally. In general, the person who has the strongest quitting point, or the ability to quit less, will have more success.

For example, when a class goes from junior high football to freshman football, many students fall out and don't go out for football. This is their quitting point. Others may play freshman football, continue on to varsity football through their senior year, and go on to college, but not play football in college. This is their quitting point. Quitting points are not good or bad, but they are important to identify. If you have an interest that you want to expand and improve, then you need to expand your quitting point. In order to achieve your goal, you must not listen to negative comments by other people or thoughts in your head about quitting.

In coaching, it is important to recognize the quitting points of athletes. A coach can expand their quitting points (physical or mental) by taking them to that point and guiding them one step beyond it. It is imperative that coaches recognize when athletes are pushed past their quitting points and reach a level of negative frustration. The athletes can then be brought back into their comfort zones. This helps the athletes expand their tolerance and realize they can accomplish things they did not believe they could. When this process is repeated, it will produce confident people who are more likely to accept challenges that previously seemed insurmountable to them. It also can solidify the coach-athlete relationship. They will come to trust and believe in each other.

Conversely, if athletes are pushed too far beyond their quitting points and their frustration levels become too high, their quitting points can actually be lowered. If athletes become too frustrated, they may believe their goals are unreachable and they are destined to fail no matter how hard they try. This can quickly sour the athlete's attitude. It is absolutely necessary that athletes see and believe that what they are doing will actually make them better. "We don't need to do this; what are we doing this for?" are examples of statements by frustrated athletes. This can destroy coach-player trust and replace it with resentment and distrust. If an athlete believes a coach is setting goals that can never be achieved, the coach is seen as a bully, rather than a mentor who is interested in the athlete's success.

Quitting points are also found in families, careers, and many other relationships. Expanding quitting points will assist in expanding positive relationships.

Examples of real-life applications:

Instructor: Give an example of how this lesson could apply to your life, family, or job.

How does expanding your quitting point apply to you?

How could expanding your quitting point apply to a team or group?

How could you apply expanding your quitting point in school or on the job?

How could you apply expanding your quitting point at your home?

How could you apply expanding your quitting point to your life in the future?

# Lesson Twenty-nine: Passion

*Hard work sometimes comes from passion, but passion more often comes from hard work.*

Explanation:

Passion is an intense emotion of enthusiasm.

It is a burning internal desire that will assist you in bringing the situation (game, practice career, or life) to the next level of intensity.

Passion brings your *all*.

It is passion that lets you give 110 percent.

It is passion that lets you leave it all on the field of competition.

It is passion that gives you the ability to practice and continue to master the fundamentals so you can expand your game or your life.

It is passion that changes a good person to a great person and a good team to a great team.

What are you passionate about? By understanding this, you will be able to use passion to your advantage in whatever you choose to do.

Examples of real-life applications:

Instructor: Give an example of how this lesson could apply to your life, family, or job.

How does passion apply to you?

How could passion apply to a team or group?

How could you apply passion in school or on the job?

How could you apply passion at your home?

How could you apply passion to your life in the future?

# Lesson Thirty: Choices

*Our lives are determined by choice, not chance.*

Explanation:

We all make choices on a daily basis; some are easy, and some are more difficult. The choices we make establish our reputations and our characters. Our characters are the most important qualities we will ever own. Our reputations are how other people perceive us, but our characters are how we perceive ourselves. When making hard choices, consider the consequences. Weigh out the positives and negatives, and then make your choice.

There is a story of a group of high school football players. This was the team that had it all. They were rated number one. They had speed, strength, size, and a great coach. They had the total package. The night before they left for their senior year playoff run, they decided to have a beer party to celebrate their success. Needless to say, police officers broke up the beer party. The following day, they had to forfeit the game that they had been working toward for many years. They did not have enough players eligible to play.

What choices did these players make? Did they consider all the people they would affect by their choices? Did they consider:

1.  The time the coach put into planning for this special game?
2.  The time their parents put in by taking them to and from practices, camps, weight-lifting sessions, and team-building events?
3.  The money their parents spent on camps, clothing, shoes, and gear?
4.  The disappointment of their teachers, fans, and other school representatives?
5.  The time and sacrifice that was spent preparing food for their pre-game and post-game meals?
6.  The time, energy, and cost of preparing the fields they practiced and played on?

7. The time and effort spent washing their uniforms so they could look classy?
8. The time spent cleaning the locker room so they could have a quality place to prepare for practices and games?
9. The young people who looked up to and idolized them?

This is just a small list of the people affected by their choices.

What happens when young athletes make bad choices? Choices affect others, and sometimes they affect the entire community. Some choices affect more people than others. When making your choices, make sure you consider all those who could possibly be affected. Make the right choice, even when it is the hard choice. This is not always easy, but the right choice is a direct result of your character.

It is extremely important to be "at choice." Being at choice means you are in control of developing your life and not just blindly following others. You are the only person responsible for your life and your level of success. To be at choice means *you* are making *your own* choices. To be at choice means *you* are responsible for developing your character and your life.

Example of real-life applications:

Instructor: Give an example of how this lesson could apply to your life, family, or job.

How could the lesson of choices apply to you?

How could the lesson of choices apply to a team or group?

How could you apply the lesson of choices in school or on the job?

How could you apply the lesson of choices at your home?

How could you apply the lesson of choices to your life in the future?

# Lesson Thirty-one: Character

*It has been said that difficult times build character; I feel that difficult times reveal character.*

Explanation:

Your character is the sum of your individual qualities and traits. Your character is how you react to different situations; your reputation is how others see you. Your character and reputation are based on the choices you make. Your character is how you see yourself; your reputation is how people interpret your behavior. Are you honest, giving, helpful, truthful, and humble? Or are you a dishonest, arrogant, or a bully?

*Your character is built by what you stand for; your reputation is built by what you fall for.*

Project

List three character traits you like in others:

1. _____
2. _____
3. _____

List three character traits you dislike in others:

1. _____
2. _____
3. _____

List three character traits you like about yourself:

1. _____
2. _____
3. _____

List three of your character traits you would like to improve in yourself:

1. _____
2. _____
3. _____

Examples of real-life applications:

Instructor: Give an example of how this lesson could apply to your life, family, or job.

How does character apply to you?

How could character apply to a team or group?

How could you apply character in school or on the job?

How could you apply character at your home?

How could you apply character to your life in the future?

*Ability can take us to the top, but it takes character to keep us there.*

# Lesson Thirty-two: *Work Ethic*

*Determination and persistence are two keys to working through failure and hardship and achieving success.*

*People and circumstances can stop you temporarily. You are the only one who can stop yourself permanently.*

Explanation:

Determination is the ability to accomplish what is necessary in order to reach your goal, executing what you know needs to be done even when you don't feel like doing it. It is being dedicated enough to achieve what you have set out to accomplish, even if it becomes difficult. This is your work ethic.

In life, I like to explain work ethic with a container and grains of sand. The container is your individual potential. Everyone's container is a different size and shape, demonstrating that everyone's potential is different in different areas of life. Some may be gifted in math and science while others maybe gifted in working on cars, building a home or in athletics. Each time you work to make yourself better in an area, you put one small grain of sand in your container. The goal is to first identify your potential and second is to work on it. The goal is to have your container (potential) as full as possible—to reach your maximum potential at any given time. This means that the harder you work, the better you can be. Therefore, how good you are now has no relationship to how good you can be when you dedicate yourself to getting better. Such is life: the harder you work on any skill, the better you will be in the future.

Understand that being self-disciplined, dedicated, and having a strong work ethic will get the maximum out of your life's potential.

Examples of real-life applications:

Instructor: Give an example of how this lesson could apply to your life, family, or job.

How does a strong work ethic apply to you?

How could a strong work ethic apply to a team or group?

How could you apply a strong work ethic in school or on the job?

How could you apply a strong work ethic at your home?

How could you apply a strong work ethic to your life in the future?

# Lesson Thirty-three: The Power of the Compliment

*The best way to stop a negative behavior is to give a pat on the back.*
*A sincere compliment is one of the most effective motivational tools in existence.*

Explanation:

A compliment is a verbal expression of courteous praise; it shows respect. To *compliment* is to recognize the good in others and, most importantly, tell them. It is best to also tell the people close to them.

Be loud with compliments and quiet with criticism.

Compliments build momentum for the player and the team.

Compliments feel good to give and to receive.

Everyone likes to receive compliments, but few people give them. I am not sure why this is. I feel great giving someone a compliment. Some people think that paying someone a compliment could bring out arrogance in the person receiving the compliment, but giving a compliment actually creates positive feelings for the giver *and* receiver. Remember the Spiritual Law of Success: everything you do comes back to you. If you want to get compliments, then give them freely, genuinely, and unconditionally.

Let's try to understand how to give and receive a compliment. To give a verbal compliment:

- Look the person directly in the eye and offer a firm handshake at the same time (if appropriate). Compliment the person with a warm tone of voice and a sincere look on your face.

To receive a verbal compliment:

- *Do one thing and one thing only: say, "Thank you," in a sincere, humble voice.*
- *Do not* come up with excuses about how you could have done better.
- *Do not* belittle your performance.
- *Do not* ignore the compliment.
- Simply acknowledge the compliment in a polite manner.

By coming up with excuses, belittling your performance, or ignoring the compliment, you make the giver of the compliment feel badly. They took the time to recognize you, so thank and respect them. Even if you were not happy with your performance, they were!

A written compliment can be a quick note or card recognizing a good act or trait or showing your appreciation for another person's talents. Make sure to sign it.

Project:

Get a group of people together. This could be your class, team, or family. Get a spool of yarn and a blank piece of thick construction paper with a hole in the top center. Each person will need a pen or a pencil. Write your name at the top of the construction paper. Put the yarn through the hole in the paper and tie it around your neck like a big necklace with the paper on your back. Then think of the nicest thing you can about each person in the room, write it on each person's paper, and sign your name. Make sure to write on everyone's paper. Do not look while others are writing; wait until you all look together. Allow time for everyone to read what the others wrote. Watch everyone smile. Have some people read their papers out loud.

Explain the emotions they may be feeling: happiness, gratitude, surprise, or appreciation. Explain how compliments can change how you look at another person or the world. Encourage everyone to keep these to read in the future. We all have greatness within us.

The construction paper can be cut into basketballs, footballs, fish, etc., to be more specific to a certain activity.

Understanding the power of the compliment can assist you a great deal in the future.

Examples of real-life applications:

Instructor: Give an example of how this lesson could apply to your life, family, or job.

Role-Playing:

Demonstrate examples of how to give and receive compliments.

Have people partner up and practice giving and receiving compliments.

How does the power of the compliment apply to you?

How could the power of the compliment apply to a team or group?

How could you apply the power of the compliment in school or on the job?

How could you apply the power of the compliment at your home?

How could you apply the power of the compliment to your life in the future?

*Doing good develops good and empowers others to do good.*
*The world needs all the good we can give.*

# Lesson Thirty-four: Honesty

*Honesty is one of the keys to getting to the top and staying there.*

Explanation:

Honesty is the ability to be truthful to yourself and others. It is important to be honest with others, but it is also important to be honest with yourself. For example, in athletics, if you're not happy with your playing time, have you done all you can to be "playable?" Have you made it to all the practices? Did you practice in the off-season? Are you doing the extra things that the others are? When something is not going your way, take a quick look within yourself to see if you can do anything to make the change. It is extremely important to be able to analyze yourself objectively and see what you have done right or wrong. Too many times, people look to blame others. When you have one finger pointing at someone else, you have three fingers pointing back at you. In life we will have the opportunity to test our honesty with our friends, parents, family, and ourselves. Make the right choice when being tested. Sometimes no one will ever know but you. It is you who is most important to you.

Examples of real-life applications:

Instructor: Give an example of how this lesson could apply to your life, family, or job.

How does honesty apply to you?

How could honesty apply to a team or group?

How could you apply honesty in school or on the job?

How could you apply honesty at your home?

How could you apply honesty to your life in the future?

*Those who lose their honesty have nothing else to lose.*

# Lesson Thirty-five: Self-confidence

*Strong self-confidence is crucial for success in life.*

*You need to understand that from this point on, your future is in capable hands—yours!*

Explanation:

Self-confidence is the ability to rely on yourself, confident that you have the capacity to make good choices and get the job done. *"If it is going to be, it is up to me."* The starting point for both success and happiness is self-confidence and a healthy self-image.

Walk with a swagger. This simply means to be confident in your abilities and/or the abilities of your team. You have learned a great deal about athletics and life. You all have a great deal of experience, thanks to your parents and all of the people who have cared enough to spend the time to teach you about life. That being said, each of you also has a lot to learn, master, and improve upon. Be confident in yourself and your team, but do not be cocky. There is an extremely fine line here. To be confident is to *"walk the walk and fill the talk."* When your self-image improves, your performance improves.

To be a great person, you must be confident in your abilities. An extremely fine line is between confidence and arrogance. This may be a difficult line to walk for some. The key factor here is the compliment. The person who can give and receive compliments in a genuine manner will have less chance of being perceived as arrogant.

When your *confidence* goes up, your *competence* goes up at the same time. To improve your self-image and self-confidence, do something nice for someone else by giving of yourself.

Examples of real-life applications:

Instructor: Give an example of how this lesson could apply to your life, family, or job.

How does self-confidence apply to you?

How could self-confidence apply to a team or group?

How could you apply self-confidence in school or on the job?

How could you apply self-confidence at your home?

How could you apply self-confidence to your life in the future?

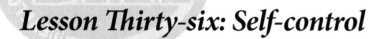

# *Lesson Thirty-six: Self-control*

*Many times the problem is not what happens to us, but how we react to what happens to us.*

Explanation:

Self-control is the ability to control our emotions, think through our options, choose the best option, and not act impulsively.

Our emotions should not control our actions. Emotional responses frequently lead to poor actions, especially if the emotions are negative, such as anger, revenge, or arrogance. Positive emotions must also be controlled to prevent the perception of arrogance or cockiness.

Self-control is a primary component to success in life.

Examples of real-life applications:

Instructor: Give an example of how this lesson could apply to your life, family, or job.

How does self-control apply to you?

How could self-control apply to a team or group?




How could you apply self-control in school or on the job?




How could you apply self-control at your home?




How could you apply self-control to your life in the future?

# Lesson Thirty-seven: Enthusiasm

*To show enthusiasm, we have to act enthusiastic. Enthusiasm is contagious.*
*Unfortunately, so is the lack of enthusiasm!*

Explanation:

The ability to be enthusiastic is the ability to celebrate loudly with great emotion. This builds the momentum for great things to happen to us and/or our team. In athletic events, great changes in momentum can make or break a team. The team that can keep and maintain positive enthusiasm is the team that will control the momentum of the game and have the advantage in the end. Celebrate loudly and with a lot of positive body language, and you and your team will have the advantage. Just as enthusiasm can bring great things to a team, it can bring great things to our lives.

Examples of real-life applications:

Instructor: Give an example of how this lesson could apply to your life, family, or job.

How does enthusiasm apply to you?

How could enthusiasm apply to a team or group?

How could you apply enthusiasm in school or on the job?

How could you apply enthusiasm at your home?

How could you apply enthusiasm to your life in the future?

# Lesson Thirty-eight: Responsibility

*We can go as far as our minds let us. What we believe, we can achieve.*

Explanation:

Responsibility is the act of being accountable for ourselves. It means having control over our actions and owning the outcome, good or bad. It is standing on our own and not blaming others for our failures. It is making our own choices and not blindly following others.

Responsibility is the key to being in charge of *your* life.

Examples of real-life applications:

Instructor: Give an example of how this lesson could apply to your life, family, or job.

How does responsibility apply to you?

How could responsibility apply to a team or group?

How could you apply responsibility in school or on the job?

How could you apply responsibility at your home?

How could you apply responsibility to your life in the future?

# Lesson Thirty-nine: Confrontation

*Our attitude toward any situation will determine our level of success or failure.*
*Our attitude will determine our altitude.*

Explanation:

To *confront* is to face or deal with a situation, problem, or issue.

Confronting another individual can be a difficult task. Mastering the ability to confront people in a productive manner will bring us success. We will have many opportunities to confront coaches, opponents, parents, and teammates when we are involved in athletic activity. For example, you may be wondering why you are not playing a certain position. You have two options. You can say nothing and just wonder, or you can confront the coach and ask why. Confrontation is not easy, but it is sometimes necessary for your questions to be answered.

Here are some guidelines to follow when confronting someone:

- It is not easy, and it's okay to be nervous.
- If you are emotional (angry or upset, for instance), do not confront the person until you have your emotions under control.
- Ask to speak with the person one-on-one in a private location. You could say something like, "I have a question I would like to ask you in private. Would tonight after practice be a good time?"
- When asking the question, be calm, confident, and unemotional. Look the person directly in the eye.
- Coach example: "John, I do not feel like you are working hard in practice. Is there something wrong that I can help you with? Is there something I can do to encourage you to work harder? When you apply yourself to your fullest, you're a talented young man. I love the way you play the game with passion and enthusiasm, when you choose to. Understand that if you choose to not practice or play to your potential, others may pass you up, and

117

you may put me in a position to find another player for your spot. I have confidence in you. All you need to do is have confidence in yourself and apply yourself. Work hard. Let's have a better practice. Any questions?"

- Athlete example: "Coach, I was playing tight end and you moved me to guard. Would you explain why? Did I do something wrong? Is there anything I can do to regain my old position?"
- When the person answers you, make eye contact and indicate that you understand or ask questions until you understand.

You may not like or agree with the answer, but at least now you understand. Now you have the opportunity to accept or debate the response until the two of you have worked this situation to a conclusion.

You may or may not like the answers you receive. However, chances are the other person will respect you for confronting the situation, and you will feel better about yourself for putting it to rest.

The example above involves sports. Please see that this can be used in any situation or relationship.

Examples of real-life applications:

Instructor: Give an example of how this lesson could apply to your life, family, or job.

How does confrontation apply to you?

How could confrontation apply to a team or group?

How could you apply confrontation in school or on the job?

How could you apply confrontation at your home?

How could you apply confrontation to your life in the future?

# Lesson Forty: *Understanding Time*

Explanation:

It is important that we understand time. Every day we have an opportunity to advance ourselves in one way or another. Every day we have an opportunity to make ourselves better or worse. Understand, we do not stay the same. Momentum is in change. Nothing sits still for very long. We are either moving up the ladder, or we are falling down the ladder. It is important to understand that many older people look back and wish they had done some things differently.

For example, a twenty-two-year-old can nolonger play high school athletics; that time has passed and is lost forever. This holds true for many different activities. Give yourself the opportunity to have many exposures in different areas, and then choose what you feel you will have success in. Remember, no hard work is ever wasted. Hard work today will help you tomorrow. Hard work today will prepare you for the opportunities of tomorrow if you are able to recognize them. If you see an opportunity and don't take advantage of it, then that time is gone. It is important to understand the concept of time; it is important to value time and not waste it.

- If you don't think a minute is important, ask a parent who has lost a child in a store and then finds the child.
- If you don't think every second is important, hold your head under water for as long as you can.
- If you don't think a hundredth of a second is important, ask the second-place finisher in an Olympic race.

*All time is important!* It is something to understand, cherish, and respect. You can waste money, and you can waste things; but don't waste time because *your time is part of your life.*

Examples of real-life applications:

**Instructor:** Give an example of how this lesson could apply to your life, family, or job.

How could understanding time apply to you?

How could understanding time apply to a team or group?

How could you apply understanding time in school or on the job?

How could you apply understanding time at your home?

How could you apply understanding time to your life in the future?

# Lesson Forty-one: Happiness

*A happy person can light up an entire room.*

Explanation:

Happiness is the ability to express pleasure or goodness. Happiness is the ability to be pleased with something and feel that pleasure internally or communicate that pleasure through words, facial expressions, or body language. Happiness is generally created by looking at the good or positive in the world around us. Some people choose not to look at the good; they only see the bad or negative. These people are generally perceived as negative or unhappy. Happiness is making the choice to look at the good around us and communicate it to others.

Project:

List five people who make you happy.

1._____

2._____

3._____

4._____

5._____

List five things that make you happy.

1._____

2._____

3._____

4._____

5._____

Happiness is not something you find; it is something you create. Happiness is how we think and how we look at the world—not what we have or what we become. Happiness is contagious; unfortunately, so is the lack of it. People are as happy as they choose to be.

Examples of real-life applications:

Instructor: Give an example of how this lesson could apply to your life, family, or job.

How does happiness apply to you?

How could happiness apply to a team or group?

How could you apply happiness in school or on the job?

How could you apply happiness at your home?

How could you apply happiness to your life in the future?

# Lesson Forty-two: Visualization

Explanation:

*Visualization* is a training technique that is used by many successful people. Visualization is the concept of vividly imagining a goal that you want to accomplish. It is a learned trait that recruits your senses so you can see, hear, smell, and feel what it is like to be there performing the task. It is theorized that training your mind is as important as training your body. This is easily performed by sitting in a quiet place, closing your eyes, and picturing yourself performing an activity as vividly as possible. This can apply to any event.

For this example, picture yourself shooting a basketball. See the ball in your hands. Feel the ball in your hands. See yourself in proper shooting form. See yourself shooting the ball with proper follow-through, and see the ball going through the hoop. Hear the ball swish through the net and bounce off the floor. Smell the gym that you are in. Picture players on the floor and fans in the stands. Visualize as many specific details as you possibly can. Picture it perfectly. If you do not picture it perfectly, or if you visualize any negative results, replay the scene without the negative results. Picture it perfectly over and over again.

This can be used for any activity, task, or situation at any time.

Visualization is a way to train your mind to help you develop success. It is important to train both mind and body.

Examples of real-life applications:

Instructor: Give an example of how this lesson could apply to your life, family, or job.

How could visualization apply to you?

How could visualization apply to a team or group?

How could you apply visualization in school or on the job?

How could you apply visualization at your home?

How could you apply visualization to your life in the future?

# *Lesson Forty-three: Responding to Negativity*

*There is power in words—what we say is what we get.*

Explanation:

Like a gate holding back an excited horse at the start of a race, negativity holds back the success that could be achieved in many activities and in life. Negativity can lead to failure. Negativity has two heads. One is the negative comment, and the other is the negative response to that comment. The best response to any negative comment is *no response*. By not responding, the negative comment has nowhere to go. Making no response is like throwing water on the fire. Giving a negative response is like throwing gas on the fire. Remember, the best response to negativity is no response. Look the person directly in the eyes, keep your mouth shut, and walk away.

Mastering the ability to not respond negativity will help you a great deal in life. If we could kick the person in the seat of the pants who is responsible for most of our troubles, we would not be able to sit down for weeks. The problem is not what happens to us, but *how* we respond to what happens to us.

Examples of real-life applications:

Instructor: Give an example of how this lesson could apply to your life, family, or job.

How does responding to negativity apply to you?

How could responding to negativity apply to a team or group?

How could you apply responding to negativity in school or on the job?

How could you apply responding to negativity at your home?

How could you apply responding to negativity to your life in the future?

# Lesson Forty-four: Dealing with Jealousy

Explanation:

Dealing with jealousy can be very difficult for both the gifted person and the less-talented person. Many pressures come with success. For an athlete who is very talented in a particular sport, jealousy may develop among other athletes or those athletes' parents. The talented athlete's parents may appear to be very proud of their child. This can be offensive to the parents whose athlete may not be in the spotlight. The less-talented athlete (or the athlete's parents) may become jealous of the other athlete's success. In turn, this may start a pattern of belittling, pointing out weaknesses in, and degrading the talented athlete. This can destroy a team from within. One of the best ways to combat this is to be certain that the talented athlete and his or her parents recognize the *good* in the other athletes around them—and then let them know how they feel! This comes down to the compliment. After receiving compliments from gifted players, less talented players (and their parents) will be less inclined to become envious. This will lead to more team support and less team division.

Realize we are *not* created equal. That is the beauty of life. Some people are great at fixing cars; others are great at fixing people. Focus on what you have to offer. Being jealous of others is a negative trait that will only bring you down. Some are more gifted in some areas than others. We all have strengths and weaknesses. Develop your strengths and strengthen your weaknesses.

Examples of real-life applications:

Instructor: Give an example of how this lesson could apply to your life, family, or job.

How does dealing with jealousy apply to you?

How could dealing with jealousy apply to a team or group?

How could you apply dealing with jealousy in school or on the job?

How could you apply dealing with jealousy at your home?

How could you apply dealing with jealousy to your life in the future?